The
Ungentlemanly
Art

The Ungentlemanly Art

A History of American Political Cartoons

by
Stephen Hess and Milton Kaplan

The Macmillan Company
New York

Collier-Macmillan Ltd.
London

JAN 1 7 1969

THE MACMILLAN COMPANY, NEW YORK

COLLIER-MACMILLAN CANADA LTD.,
TORONTO, ONTARIO

PRINTED IN THE UNITED STATES OF AMERICA

For
Charles Phillip Hess
James Randall Hess

and
Gail Alaine Kaplan
Linda Marlene Kaplan

Our special reasons for
recalling that laughter
is part of
the American legacy

Contents

The
Ungentlemanly
Art

"WHO STOLE THE PEOPLE'S MONEY?" — DO TELL. N.Y.TIMES.   'TWAS HIM.

I-1

I

"Them Damn Pictures"

"STOP THEM DAMN PICTURES," demanded William Marcy Tweed of his henchmen. "I don't care so much what the papers write about me. My constituents can't read. But, damn it, they can see pictures."

This outburst was inspired by a cartoon in the August 19, 1871, issue of *Harper's Weekly,* in which the obese boss of Tammany and his three chief cohorts — Peter B. (Brains) Sweeny, Richard B. (Slippery Dick) Connolly, and New York Mayor A. Oakey (O.K.) Hall—are shown pointing to one another in response to the question "Who stole the people's money?" Their theft was estimated at $200 million, and Tweed asked the reformers, "As long as I count the votes, what are you going to do about it?"

A thirty-one-year-old German-born cartoonist, Thomas Nast, was trying to do something about it, and Tweed wanted him stopped. A Tammany banker was sent to Nast's home with an offer of $100,000 if he would "study art" in Europe.

"Do you think I could get *two* hundred thousand?" asked the $5,000-a-year artist.

"Well, possibly. . . . You have a great talent."

Curious to see how high a price his talent commanded, the cartoonist bid up Tweed's emissary to a half-million dollars. Then, according to his biographer, Nast said, "I don't think I'll go to Europe. I made up my mind not long ago to put some of those fellows behind bars, and I'm going to put them there."

Nast's subsequent campaign against the Tweed Ring, the most brilliant in the history of American political cartooning, is reserved for later in our story. But the result should be noted here.

On July 1, 1876, Nast pictured Tweed in a prison-stripe suit holding two street urchins by their collars. The point of the cartoon was that the Tweed Ring's self-proclaimed reformation consisted of nothing more than arresting the most humble culprits while the major criminals remained at large. The drawing was not one of Nast's most felicitous efforts. Yet it did contain a good likeness of Tweed, who had fled to Spain.

Soon after, a cable from Vigo, Spain, stated that "Twid" had been apprehended for kidnaping two American children. "This seemed a curious statement," wrote Albert Bigelow Paine, "for whatever may have been the Boss's sins, he had not been given to child-stealing."

What happened was that a Spanish official who did not read English had spotted Tweed from the *Harper's Weekly* cartoon, and, while he assumed the wrong crime, his identification was

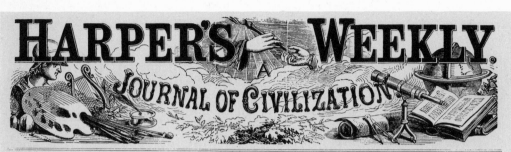

Vol. XX.—No. 1018.]   NEW YORK, SATURDAY, JULY 1, 1876.   [WITH A SUPPLEMENT. PRICE TEN CENTS.

Entered according to Act of Congress, in the Year 1876, by Harper & Brothers, in the Office of the Librarian of Congress, at Washington.

POLITICAL "CAPITAL."

THE "people are in a very puzzled and despondent state of mind about the political situation, and have got beyond the point at which they look for the appearance of the ideal statesman uniting the purest motives with the highest ability. They can get the pure motives, and they can get the high ability; but somehow, owing to no matter what circumstances, to get a man who unites both into a leading place in the government is a work of such difficulty that most people have given it up as (for the present at least) a bad job, and are willing to content themselves with any man who, for whatever motive, will do good work. It so happens, too, that the work to be done at this moment is not work which calls either for the highest order of genius or the highest aspirations. A man may do it very well without being a Moses or a Washington—without, in short, being either a prophet or a hero. He has neither to lead a race out of captivity nor call a nation into existence. The task before the American politician of to-day is the simple and somewhat homely one of preventing public officers from stealing and dividing the public money, and of preventing the government from cheating its creditors; and when a man offers himself for this work, there is no general disposition to ask whether he is a statesman of the first rank, or whether his political judgment has always been sure or his voice been always heard on the right side. In fact, they go so far as to say that to make capital in this way is a good thing to do, and they wish all politicians to engage in it. They are ready to forbear all curious inquiries into the motives or antecedents of men who will undertake to put an end to cheating and stealing. In fact, the voters of the country are sticking notices up offering the highest offices in their gift, and "no questions asked," to any body who will bring in a few plunderers of the state. Mr. TILDEN has achieved his present success simply owing to his having, before any body else of his class, understood the exact nature of the situation. He perceived sooner than his competitors that the time had come to stop preaching, and to begin making arrests and drawing up indictments. He now finds, and his competitors find, that his acuteness has rendered him the highest service, and his enemies actually play into his hands."—*The Nation*, October 7, 1875.

Text within the cartoon:

IT HAS BLOWN OVER.

WANTED REFORMERS OF THE TAMMANY CLASS.

WANTED REFORMERS EDUCATED IN THE TAMMANY HALL SCHOOL OF REFORM.

REFORM

REFORMED THIEVES WANTED TO TAKE CARE OF THE PEOPLE'S MONEY.

REWARD AND NO QUESTIONS ASKED.

ANYBODY WHO WILL BRING A FEW PLUNDERERS OF THE STATE TO JUSTICE (?) WILL BE REWARDED BY THE HIGHEST OFFICES IN THE GIFT OF THE PEOPLE.

C.D. LORD CONVICTED. ONE OF THE CANAL RING.

TAMMANY HALL SCHOOL OF REFORM. SCHOLARS WANTED FOR REFORMERS.

REWARD TO THOSE THAT HAVE ASSOCIATED WITH THIEVES, AND WILL GIVE STATE EVIDENCE.

TAMMANY POLICE. RING

REWARD TO ALL PUBLIC THIEVES WHO HAVE ENOUGH AND CAN STOP OTHERS FROM CHEATING AND STEALING. THEY WILL BE REWARDED BY HONORABLE POSITIONS AND FAT OFFICES.

IT TAKES A THIEF OR ONE WHO HAS ASSOCIATED WITH THIEVES TO CATCH A THIEF.

Th:Nast.

TWEED-LE-DEE AND TILDEN-DUM.

REFORM TWEED. "If all the people want is to have somebody arrested, I'll have you plunderers convicted. You will be allowed to escape; nobody will be hurt; and then TILDEN will go to the White House, and I to Albany as Governor."

flawless. Ironically, Tweed's baggage was found to contain a complete set of Nast's cartoons except for the one that was to send him to jail.

Boss Tweed died on April 12, 1878, in Ludlow Street Jail, New York City, where he occupied the warden's parlor at $75 a week.[1]

Although Nast's crusade against the Tweed Ring might have been the most dramatic instance of cartooning on the American continent, men have been producing "them damn pictures" ever since some stone-age Herblock scratched an irreverent representation of a tribal chief on his cave wall. Some say the oldest extant cartoon is of Ikhnaton, the unpopular father-in-law of King Tutankhamen, and dates about 1360 B.C. "Ikhnaton's features, however," writes Isabel Simeral Johnson, "were so abnormally ugly that it is difficult to tell a caricature of him from an authentic portrait."[2] But it seems beyond doubt that the Roman soldier at Pompeii who drew an unflattering portrait of some long-forgotten centurion on the wall of his barracks was a political cartoonist—that is, he was pictorially making a political statement.

Charting the route of caricature from the shadow of Vesuvius in the first century to mid-eighteenth century Philadelphia, where a printer named Benjamin Franklin designed the first American political cartoon, one travels by way of Pieter Brueghel's Flanders, seventeenth-century Holland, and the

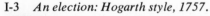

I-3 *An election: Hogarth style, 1757.*

London of William Hogarth. "How I want thee, humorous Hogarth," mused Jonathan Swift in a poem ending:

Draw them so that we may trace
All the soul in every face.

Like his predecessors, Hogarth was concerned more with affairs social than political. Even his great series "The Elections" was only a highly generalized comment on politics.[3]

The raw, robust artistry of Hogarth and his fellow Englishmen—Henry Bunbury, Thomas Rowlandson, Isaac Cruikshank—would turn the eighteenth century into "the century of caricature," and their work could hardly have failed to be noted by the Crown's colonists across the Atlantic. But for sheer impact on the emerging American cartoonists none was the equal of James Gillray, the first master draftsman to devote himself to the regular production of political satires. Gillray, unlike Hogarth, could not have been more specific as one sees in his drawings of the Empress Josephine dancing naked before Barras while Napoleon watches through a curtain or of Bonaparte skewered and toasted as a meal for Beelzebub in hell.[4] The compositions of the first major American cartoonist to work on American soil, William Charles, would be in rank imitation of this genius.

Even the word "cartoon" is part of America's debt to its mother country. Gillray's work was known as "carica-ture." At the time "cartoon" meant no more than the preliminary sketch for a fresco or painting. But when in July, 1843, the British government held an exhibition of cartoons that had been commissioned to beautify the houses of Parliament, the humor magazine *Punch*, feeling that there were better uses for the money, published a picture of a ragged crowd inspecting a gallery of elegant paintings. And this "Cartoon No. 1," as the John Leech drawing was titled, made an unexpected contribution to the English language.

At first merely a weak carbon copy of the European model, American cartooning displayed only modest wit and originality until well into the Civil War–Reconstruction periods. Even then the leading American artists—Nast; Frank Bellew, first of the great magazine cartoonists; the Confederate Adalbert Volck; Matt Morgan, brought from Lon-

I-4   *Gillray sees himself as the Devil, 1788.*

don to draw for *Frank Leslie's Illustrated Newspaper;* Joseph Keppler, founder of *Puck;* Bernard Gillam of the rival *Judge*—were foreign-born and, in some cases, foreign trained. In fact, it was not until James A. Wales of Clyde, Ohio, joined *Wild Oats* in 1873 that the United States produced a home-bred political cartoonist of the first order.[5]

If Americans were artistic laggards during the eighteenth and much of the nineteenth century, they were also instinctively political and generally blessed with an appreciation of the ridiculous. Thus when native cartoonists finally blossomed, they were well rooted in friendly soil, and the bountiful harvest included such names as Homer Davenport, Frederick Opper, John McCutcheon, and Art Young.

American cartoonists have been a varied lot. The Boston *Post's* Norman Ritchie was ambidextrous, drawing equally well with either hand. Tom Vidro of the Grand Rapids *Press* had only one finger on his drawing hand, a

I-5   *Commenting on the first political "cartoon" in 1843,* Punch *wrote, "The poor ask for bread and the philanthrophy of the State accords an exhibition."*

chain saw having removed the others; he manipulated his pen with thumb and the fleshy part of the hand.[6] In 1924 editor Hugh S. Fullerton recalled having roomed with a cartoonist (unnamed) who used to lie nude in bed holding a sheet of paper against the wall with one foot while drawing a cartoon with a pencil held between the toes of the other foot. "He used to explain that he might some day lose both arms in a railroad accident. . . ."[7] T. E. Powers, a first-rate artist of the "tickle-'em-to-death" school, kept a bear in the backyard of his Washington Square townhouse. All of which probably means that practitioners of political cartooning are only slightly more eccentric than other mortals.

Some cartoonists, like other mortals, have chosen their profession because it was their fathers.' This, too, is an English tradition: the Cruikshanks and the Doyles, for example. Frank Bellew's son used "Chip" as an artistic signature in recognition, no doubt, of his "old block." The most famous father-son cartooning team in the United States during the nineteenth century was the Joseph Kepplers, Senior and Junior. (The younger Keppler was christened Udo but changed his name after his sire's death.) Clifford K. Berryman, the Washington Star's cartoonist from 1908 until he died in 1949, was the son of a crossroads merchant who spent his spare time caricaturing his customers on wrapping paper. When Cliff Berryman collapsed on May 29, 1935, while drawing a Memorial Day cartoon, his son James was called from the Star's art department (where he was "drawing pots and pans and stuff like that") to finish his father's work. He continued to draw for the editorial page until his own retirement on January 1, 1965. The Berryman's, pere et fils, were awarded Pulitzer Prizes.[8] Shaw McCutcheon, cartoonist for the Spokesman Review (Spokane, Washington), is the son of John T. McCutcheon; while another son, Barr, is a conservative Chicago Chicago alderman, a position that also befits an offspring of the great Chicago Tribune artist. In Memphis, an Alley, either the late J. P. or his son Cal, has been the cartoonist for the Commercial Appeal almost without a break since 1914. In all cases—Berrymans, McCutcheons, and Alleys—the styles of the sons have not been radically different from their fathers'.

The Gillam brothers, Bernard and Victor, were the artistic mainstays of Judge, and the Baltimore Sunpapers once had McKee Barclay drawing political cartoons for its morning paper and his brother Thomas, under the pen name "Tom Bee," as his counterpart on the Evening Sun. The cartoonists for the Nashville Tennessean, Tom Little and Charles Bissell, are brothers-in-law.

Nearly ten years after Clare Briggs's death in 1930, his popular When a Fel-

ler Needs a Friend began to reappear; this time it was drawn by Miss Clare Briggs, the originator's daughter. Generally, however, cartooning has been a man's world. One hardly needs more than the normal number of fingers to count the lady political cartoonists. They include Alice McKee; Lou Rogers; Emma M. Gordon; Edwina Dumm, who left the Columbus (Ohio) *Daily Monitor* to start the successful *Cap Stubbs and Tippie* comic strip; Anne Mergen, whose cartoons helped the Miami *Daily News* win a Pulitzer Prize in 1939; and Fay King, an artist for the Denver *Post* and later the San Francisco *Examiner* but better known in her day for a marriage to and rapid divorce from "Battling" Nelson, the lightweight boxing champion.

Besides gender, one of the few things that most American cartoonists have had in common is a lack of artistic training. Paradoxically, this may have been a strength of the profession, thought John Ames Mitchell, a founder of the old *Life* magazine and himself a cartoonist. "It is a melancholy fact," he wrote in 1889, "that the tendency of an artistic education is to tone down and frequently eliminate, in a majority of students, that playfulness and fancy which are often the very life of a drawing."[9]

The problem, in part, is that few schools have offered meaningful instruction for the would-be political cartoonist. Notable exceptions have been Boardman Robinson's class at the Art Students' League of New York, whose graduates included Edmund Duffy, Ross Lewis, Jacob Burck, and Art Birnbaum; and, more recently, the class of Vaughn Shoemaker at the Chicago Academy of Fine Arts, where such stalwarts as Bill Mauldin, Dan Dowling, Ed Holland, Cal Alley, Charles Brooks, and Art Poinier have been taught the rudiments of their trade.

Yet, perhaps more basically, it was the very artlessness of a Walt McDougall or later of a "Ding" Darling that lay at the heart of their humor. Frederick Opper, long a thoroughbred in *Puck's* stable, was so unaware of basic anatomy that one of his cartoons showed a skeleton with two bones in its upper arm.[10] Even Nast, the American who made the most lasting contribution to the medium, was a less than superb

I-6 *One of the few lady cartoonists draws a self-portrait.*

draftsman. Fellow cartoonist Frank Beard commented that Nast failed to infuse individuality into any part of his subjects except their faces. "His fat men are all alike below the shirt collar." Not only were they cast from the same mold, but Nast sent them to the same tailor.[11]

There have been significant exceptions, of course. Such outstanding artists as George Luks and John Sloan of the famous "ash-can school," Reginald Marsh, and Ben Shahn have all produced political cartoons.

I-7 *George Luks, 1899.*

HANNA: THAT MAN CLAY WAS AN ASS. IT'S BETTER TO BE PRESIDENT THAN TO BE RIGHT!

(Lyonel Feininger, the expressionist, employed his artistic technique in a Sunday comic strip for the Chicago *Tribune*, which he signed "Your Uncle Feininger.")[12]

One of the finest American newspaper cartoonists during the years be-tween the World Wars, Rollin Kirby, may have solved this paradox when he said in 1918 that a good cartoon consists of 75 per cent *idea* and 25 per cent *drawing*. "A good idea has carried many an indifferent drawing to glory," commented Kirby, "but never has a good

I-8   *John Sloan, 1914.*

IN THIS ISSUE
CLASS WAR IN COLORADO—Max Eastman
WHAT ABOUT MEXICO?—John Reed

drawing rescued a bad idea from oblivion."[13]

Oddly enough, the creativity curve of cartoonists more closely resembles that of the physicist than of the philosopher. Advanced age may increase wisdom, but it decreases the likelihood that a man will make a great scientific breakthrough or a stirring political cartoon. Thomas Nast was thirty-one when he took on Boss Tweed, and he had already been the nation's leading political artist for seven years. Cartoonists may very well become more proficient draftsmen in their later years, but, by and large, the history of their art shows that they are also likely to begin repeating themselves and, more importantly, may lose the crusading spirit that is part of youth's zeal.

Although a great cartoon fuses memorable art and idea—each reinforcing the other—it is possible to produce an often-adequate cartoon without real artistic ability, and thus the ranks of social and political cartoonists have been filled with some inspired amateurs, starting, at least, with a priest named Martin Luther. Many of these Sunday cartoonists have been writers of note: William Makepeace Thackeray, Mark Twain, O. Henry, G. K. Chesterton, Hendrik Willem Van Loon. Even "Dr. Seuss" put aside the stories of *Horton the Elephant* and *The Cat in the Hat* to draw some telling political cartoons for *PM*, a short-lived New York daily. But possibly the most inspired amateur was the great Neapolitan tenor Enrico Caruso, whose caricatures were a regular feature for eighteen years of *La Follia*, a weekly Italian language newspaper in New York.

On the other hand, professional cartoonists have not been shy about trying their hands at a variety of occupational

Fresh, spirited American troops, flushed with victory, are bringing in thousands of hungry, ragged, battle-weary prisoners. (News item)

I-9 *Sergeant Bill Mauldin was only twenty-three years old when he was awarded the Pulitzer Prize in 1945 for this* Stars & Stripes *cartoon. According to the artist, General George S. Patton called him to headquarters and accused him of "undermining the morale of the Army, destroying the confidence in the command [and], making soldiers unsoldierly."*

WILLIAM III.,
King of Prussia.

I-10 *Mark Twain, 1871.*
Twain's caricature of His Majesty
"William III, King of Prussia" (William
I of Germany), was meant to satirize the
quality of the artwork in Galaxy
magazine. "I never can look at those
periodical portraits in the Galaxy," wrote
Twain, "without feeling a wild,
tempestuous ambition to become an
artist."

I-11 *O. Henry, 1894.*
The two-horse rider, Charles A.
Culberson, a candidate for governor of
Texas, appeared on the cover of a weekly
magazine that was owned and edited for a
year by O. Henry while he was an Austin
bank clerk. It was the profession of
banking, not cartooning, that led to his
imprisonment.

I-12 *Enrico Caruso, 1908.*
This caricature of Theodore
Roosevelt was one of the thousands
that Caruso contributed without pay
to La Follia di New York, *although,
according to the paper's publisher,
the singer rejected an offer of
$50,000 a year to draw for Pulitzer's
World.*

sidelines, too. One of them even got himself elected to Congress. John M. Baer, cartoonist for the North Dakota Nonpartisan League, was elected to the House of Representatives for the first of two terms in 1917.[14] (Another cartoonist-congressman, Robert Eckhardt, must be put in the "inspired amateur" class. A Houston attorney, who was elected to the House of Representatives in 1966, Eckhardt had been the car-

toonist for the weekly *Texas Spectator* [1945-1948], a spiritual heir to O. Henry's *The Rolling Stone.*) And "Pitchfork Ben" Tillman, the fiery senator from South Carolina, although not a cartoonist, did "design" a cartoon of a gigantic cow straddling the United States with her head being fed by the farmers of the West while a Wall Street capitalist milked her in the East. After an artist made a rendering of the idea, Tillman put it in the *Congressional Record,* an unprecedented event, which, according to the Washington *Post,* "created a flurry at the Capitol."[15]

A number of cartoonists have also turned to serious writing, with varying results. George du Maurier is today better remembered for the novel *Trilby* than for the satires on the upper class

I-13　*John M. Baer, the cartoonist-congressman, 1918. Baer apparently did not consider it* infra dig *to draw a critical cartoon of the Senate while serving in the House. He was first elected with the help of fellow cartoonists on a platform that promised— undoubtedly with tongue in cheek—to introduce legislation to compel editors to put cartoons on page one.*

that he drew for *Punch*. Currently, James Stevenson, the talented *New Yorker* cartoonist, has published four novels, and Jules Feiffer had a play on Broadway in 1967 despite the warnings of his friends, who, he said, suggested that "while I was skilled at my usual profession of drawing one anti-American cartoon a week, if I ventured into the field of anti-American plays I'd be in danger of spreading myself thin."[16] New York critics agreed with the syndicated cartoonist's friends.

There has also been an interrelationship between the professions of acting and cartooning. John Barrymore, Peter Ustinov and comedian Jonathan Winters have produced some amusing pictures. (One of the latter's shows an elephant saying to another elephant, "Would you believe it, Fred, I'm a Democrat?") Cartoonists who have had a fling at acting include David Claypoole Johnston, Joseph Keppler, and Bill Mauldin. "I think that whatever taste or ability I may have in the way of color and composition," Keppler once remarked, "is due in great measure to the theatre with its arrangements of groups and its decorative and scenic effects."

Feiffer is one of the rare political cartoonists who began their career drawing for comic books. But ever since the inauguration of the newspaper comic strip in the 1890s, a steady stream of political cartoonists have switched over to the comic page, among them: Clare Briggs (*Mr. and Mrs., When a Feller Needs a Friend*), R. M. Brinkerhoff (*Little Mary Mixup*), Billy De Beck (*Barney Google*), Fontaine Fox (*Toonerville Trolley*), Winsor McCay (*Little Nemo*), Jimmy Murphy (*Toots and Casper*), Frederick Opper (*Happy Hooligan*), and H. T. Webster (*The Timid Soul*.)[17] The obvious reason for this migration is money. A popular comic strip, such as Bud Fisher's *Mutt and Jeff*, could earn for its creator a yearly income of a quarter of a million dollars, while possibly the highest-paid political cartoonist in the history of the art, Homer Davenport, was paid considerably less, reportedly $1000 a week.[18]

Several artists, such as Tom Little of the Nashville *Tennessean* and Cecil Jensen of the Chicago *Daily News*, have done editorial cartoons and comic strips at the same time. But the only major figure ever to move completely from the comics to political cartooning is Rube Goldberg, the majestic inventor. In his second career he would win a Pulitzer Prize and yet fail to equal the heights of imagination that had earlier turned his name into an adjective (*Goldbergian:* grotesquely complex; contrived with inept and excessive intricacy).[19]

If the movement of talent has often been from political cartoons to comic strips, there has also been a counter-movement from the sports page to the editorial page. Among the political cartoonists who first drew sports cartoons have been Burris Jenkins, Jr. (New York *Journal-American*), William Crawford (Newark *News*, Newspaper Enterprise Association), and Karl Hubenthal (Los Angeles *Herald-Examiner*).

The relationship between the comics and politics goes beyond—but may have been carried over from—the artists who got their start on the editorial page. In fact, Richard F. Outcault, inventor of the first successful comic strip, *The Yellow Kid*, laced the doings in his Hogan's Alley with a healthy dose of political comment. Even the *Little King* of O. Soglow "is a biting indictment of the job of being a king these days," wrote Rollin Kirby in 1933. "If you don't think so, look at the King of Italy."[20]

Through the years the most blatantly political of the comic strips has been *Little Orphan Annie*. Its ultra-conservative creator, Harold Gray, eschewed politics from the strip's inception in 1924 until 1934; then his strong distaste for Franklin D. Roosevelt burst onto the comic page. Gray's point of view was evident: Annie's benefactor was "Daddy" Warbucks, who, as his name implied, was a munitions tycoon if not an outright war profiteer. On July 11, 1934, Richard L. Neuberger, a liberal journalist and future U.S. senator, wrote in *The New Republic*, "At the current writing 'Daddy' Warbucks is on trial for cheating the government out of its taxes. Of course, everyone knows he is not guilty; he is being railroaded by agitating politicians, malcontents and dangerous college professors . . . while [noncoincidentally, in real life] Samuel Insull awaits trial for the collapse of his utilities empire at the hands of a government whose President is

I-14   The Yellow Kid, *1896. The first successful comic strip.*

influenced by insidious university pedagogues. . . ."[21]

Another highly political comic strip has been *Pogo*, drawn by Walt Kelly, who introduced the little opossum and his animal friends while serving as art director and political cartoonist of the ill-fated New York *Star*, 1948–49. (As a political cartoonist, Kelly's most amusing conceit was to turn Thomas E. Dewey into a mechanical man.) Over the years Kelly's *Pogo* has kidded

I-15   *This episode in* Orphan Annie *appeared in June, 1967, at the time that a "flag-burning" bill was pending in the U.S. House of Representatives. The next week it passed, making the penalty for burning an American flag "not more than $1,000 or imprisonment for not more than one year, or both."*

I-16   *In a book published in 1964 Al Capp wrote, "The main purpose of* Li'l Abner *is to make a living for me. The secondary and more celebrated purpose is to create suspicion of, and disrespect for, the perfection of all established institutions." Then in 1967, after Capp attacked the Vietnam peace marchers as "S.W.I.N.E.," he told a* Boston Globe *reporter, "The independent humorist has one function and this to attack lunacy. He attacks it wherever it is. Now for 30 years I attacked lunacy on the Right because that's where it was. . . . If it shifts from Right to Left, as it did, I simply turn my aim . . .*

I-17   *A few days after* Orphan Annie's *"flag-burning" incident, Chester Gould's* Dick Tracy *was making known his views on recent defendant-oriented opinions of the Supreme Court.*

the John Birch Society, turned Soviet Premier Krushchev into a pig and Cuban Premier Castro into a jackass, and invented a character called Simple J. Malarkey, who closely resembled a U.S. senator from Wisconsin. Said Kelly, "It was probably a surprise to a good many people to find that many aspects of Joe McCarthy were ridiculous and that fun could be derived from them in a comic strip." [22]

Obviously, then, political cartoons need not be limited to the editorial page. Packs of political playing cards were popular in seventeenth-century England, and later the English printed cartoons on ladies' fans "and other articles of similarly intimate character." [23] One early American cartoonist got even with a publisher with whom he had had a disagreement by having a caricature of his enemy reproduced on earthenware chamber pots. (The publisher and his friends bought and destroyed most of them.) [24]

In both the North and South during the Civil War, envelopes were decorated with political cartoons.

In 1896 *Leslie's Illustrated Weekly* —perhaps recalling that the great Daumier had made clay models and drawn his caricatures from them—printed photographs of clay cartoons. The experiment was revived in 1939 by Paul D. Battenfield for the Chicago *Times*.

I-18 *One West Coast newspaper editor, according to Kelly, felt that Malarkey was too heavily whiskered and had his art department give the Senator McCarthy-like character a shave.*

Kelly adopted the technique of using distinctive lettering to indicate the tone of voice. Here Deacon (a muskrat) speaks in Gothic type, while an earlier character, P. T. Bridgeport (a bear), speaks in circus-poster letters.

Music by the " Contra-Band."

Sold by S. C. Upham, 310 Chestnut St.

Deaf Man—I have got the Secession Fever, and it is making me deaf.
Union Man—Get some of Magee's Union Envelopes, and that will cure you of the fever.

I-19   *Cartoons printed on envelopes in the North during the Civil War.*

But the process was time-consuming and lacked flexibility.[25]

A more recent gimmick in political cartooning is adding captions or balloons to existing photographs.

The partisan use of cartoons by political parties and candidates has a long history. During the 1899 gubernatorial contest in Ohio, for instance, William L. Bloomer drew 150 cartoons for the Republican State Executive Committee, which were distributed in 20,000 cuts to over 125 newspapers. The committee later claimed that "99 per cent of them were used by the papers receiving the service." The Republicans won the election.[26] The Democratic National Committee hired Thomas Nast in the 1888 Presidential campaign and the Republicans hired Homer Davenport in 1904. (Both reportedly had difficulty getting paid for their work.) More recently, Republican National Chairman Guy G. Gabrielson credited a cartoon

I-20   *A clay cartoon, 1896.*

LESLIE'S WEEKLY
ILLUSTRATED

Vol. LXXXIII—No. 2146.
New York, October 1, 1896.
Price, 10 Cents.

OUR GALLERY OF STATUES—XVI.

UNITED FOR THE NATIONAL HONOR.

pamphlet, mailed to 973,000 voters in New Jersey, with carrying that state for Dewey in 1948.[27] During Nelson Rockefeller's successful gubernatorial campaign of 1966, one of his television commercials was made up entirely of cartoons of the Governor taken from New York newspapers.[28]

Commenting on the use of photographs as cartoons, Scott Long, political cartoonist for the Minneapolis *Tribune*, called them "harmless substitutes." Said Long, "The cartoonist deals with abstractions, ideas and emotions that are beyond the comprehension of a lens. The photographer deals with physical objects. Ask a photographer to take a picture of the Dollar Gap or the New Deal or the Great Leap Forward or the Wave of the Future or the Separation of Church and State or the Monroe Doctrine and he will be baffled. . . ."[29]

I-21   *The 1967 photograph of Senator Robert Kennedy was captioned by the Republican Congressional Committee.*

I-22   *The balloon on the photograph of President Eisenhower and his press secretary, James Hagerty, was provided by Gerald Gardner, who became a Kennedy campaign aide.*

JAMES K. POLK.

THE COON DISSECTOR.

JOHN ANDERSON, Editor.

"Truth crush'd to earth will rise again,
The eternal years of God are her's;
But error, wounded, writh's in pain,
And dies amid her worshippers."

DAYTON, O:
Friday, Aug. 23, 1844.

FOR PRESIDENT,
JAMES K. POLK,
OF TENNESSEE.

FOR VICE PRESIDENT,
GEO. M. DALLAS,
OF PENNSYLVANIA.

ELECTORIAL TICKET.

SENATORIAL.
Joseph H. Larwill, of Wayne,
Dowty Uter, of Clermont.

CONGRESSIONAL.

1st District,	Clayton Webb, of Hamilton,
2d "	James M. Dorsey, of Darke,
3d "	R. D. Foreman, of Greene,
4th "	Judge John Taylor, of Champaign,
5th "	David Higgins, of Lucas,
6th "	Gilbert Beach, of Wood,
7th "	John D. White, of Brown,
8th "	Thomas McGrady, of Ross,
9th "	Valentine Keller, of Pickaway,
10th "	James Parker, of Licking,
11th "	Greville P. Cherry, of Marion,
12th "	George Corwine, of Scioto,
13th "	Cautious C. Covey, of Morgan,
14th "	Isaac M. Lanning, of Guernsey,
15th "	Walter Jamieson, of Harrison,
16th "	Sebastian Brainard, of Tuscarawas,
17th "	James Forbes, er. of Carroll,
18th "	Neal McCoy, of Wayne,
19th "	Milo Stone, of Summit,
20th "	Benjamin Adams, of Lake,
21st "	Stephen N. Sargent, of Medina.

FOR GOVERNOR,
DAVID TOD,
OF TRUMBULL COUNTY.

COUNTY MASS MEETING.

DEMOCRATIC RALLY!
GEN. LEWIS CASS.

The brave defender of our Country's Rights, will address the people at Dayton *On Wednesday, the 28th of August, inst.*
HON. THOMAS L. HAMER,
HON. ALEX. DUNCAN, and
DAVID T. DISNEY, Esq.,
will be present on this occasion. The democratic candidate for Vice President,
HON. GEORGE M. DALLAS,
is to be at Massilon, in this State, on the 24th inst., and has been invited to attend.

Come up to Dayton, on that day, fellow citizens! Hear what these friends of their country, have to say for their Country's Cause.

To Correspondents.—"Truth teller" must make his manuscript more eligible and endorse. We are acquainted with some of the facts stated, but adhere to the rule.—The same will apply to Blank, relative to the Buckeye Book Binder stopping his dealings with a painter who had engaged to paint a POLK and DALLAS flag.

SPIRIT OF 1840

Clay's Apple-cart Upset.

HAVE YOU HEARD FROM KENTUCK!

"Oh Kentucky, the Heroes of Kentucky."

The above cut, comes more near the returns of the "Banner State" than all the tom fooleries of the coon Journals and Scottlanders of our city. You will observe old Harry's apple cart is upset; and the apples on which he had placed his hope are scattered to the wind; his way has been obstructed by the Texian Polk stalk, by which his *brag* coon is felled. Illinois and Alabama have put in their *rails* and have overturned all his exceptions, in the hard cider line, for four years more.—alas poor Harry. We have heard of you once going to mill with *corn* your *trousaloons* being some what worse of the journey; but now your whole suit is soiled by the dirt of the way side, and there is no more left of you to be admired but the *embodiment*,
HUZZA! HUZZA!! FOR THE DEMOCRACY!!!

SOMETHING TO CROW OVER.

LOUISIANA with her 6 electoral votes has declared for the democracy.
INDIANA presents her 12.
ILLINOIS in thunder tones proclaims her 9 for POLK and DALLAS!!!
MISSOURI! Glorious Missouri!! make way for her 9,
ALABAMA! The Praries are on fire!! Put down her 9.
KENTUCKY, the banner State before the election, with her 25000 whig majority, now, so poor, "there's none to do her reverence." Her 12 extremely doubtful.
NORTH CAROLINA put down her 11 doubtful. Strong whig before election; mighty uncertain since.
Since the nomination of Polk and Dallas, the democrats elected SIXTEEN members of Congress the whigs only TWO!!!

GLORIOUS ILLINOIS.—As we have heretofore stated, the victory of the Democracy of Illinois is overwhelming. The State Register of Friday says: "It will be seen that all the Democratic candidates for Congress are elected, except Calhoun, and that the State has gone Democratic by at least 12,000 majority."
In November the majority in Illinois will be full fifteen thousand.

ALABAMA.—The democrats have defeated federal whiggery even in its strong hold. The city of Mobile has elected a democratic senator and three delegates to one whig. The democracy have made a clean sweep.

J. W. McCorkle.—Will address the People at Johnsville, on Saturday next.

Remember the Mass Meeting on Wednesday next!

ELECTIONS.
The Democratic States. Missouri, Illinois

and Alabama have given increased majorities despite all the blustering of the Whigs. Hear what the St. Louis *New Era* a whig paper says of Missouri;—read it fellow democrats,—and show it to your whig neighbor that he may see that all the boasting of the whigs about Missouri, was all gammon,—deception.

"*Next Legislature.*—In the Senate there will be 8 whigs and 25 Locofocos. Of the Senators there may be 5 or 6 opposed to the ultra Hards; but there is a decided Hard Bentonian majority, and suppose that the Softs will generally be coaxed or whipped back into the ranks. We think that about 45 whigs will be found in the House of Representatives, and 55 Locofocos. There may be a few independents among them, but they will not be strong, and some of them will probably be recaptured by the Bentonians. From present appearances we are inclined to believe that the Bentonians will have the power on joint ballot; if so, Benton will be re-elected, and also some other subserviant Loco, who will serve as a make weight to the great humbugger. If the Bentonians carry the Legislature they will carry out Bentonian measures and policy just so far as they dare; they will possibly Gerrymander the State, but not district it, and the old corrupt Clique policy and organization will be adhered to. The softs may be stronger than we suppose, but we do not know where their members are to come from.

Later news and from a democratic paper assures us, that the majority on joint ballot will be about 20 true blue Bentonian democrats, over *softs* and *whigs* combined.

PAY UP! PAY UP!! PAY UP!!!

This being the commencement of our new series of the Dissector, we would intimate, for the first time that we cannot furnish our paper to subscribers for promise. We being known as a customer of that old adage, "Right is Right."

There are many in the adjoining counties who are in arrears, and will much oblige us by *forking over* to their several Post Masters who we flatter ourselves will remit forthwith. Those in the city can "just step in" at the office and all will be made right, before you can say *nuf-sed*.

THE WHY AND THE WHEREFORE.

The reason the Germantown Band did not come over last week with the delegation from that place was this: They (the Band) being all democrats save two, upon being seated in the Band waggon, rebelled against putting those baby hankerchief flags, of Clay and Frelinghuysen, on their horses, preferring Polk stalks. The coons insisting upon the flags being up, the Musicians dismounted un-hitched, and agreed to stay at home, and no money could induce them to ride here under coon color. Good luck!

The *Scott* land-r says, we are beneat h his notice. What a pity! Look here chappie! will you tell us something about your father having his horses shod, and his goods packed last war, ready to make a forced march with his family (including your soustoselship,) to Canada!—We have some news from Licking county which perhaps will be quite edifying to your readers. "Beneath your notice," hey! how came your eye out, hey! We spose you've heard from Licking Kentucky, and we are determined to let you hear from Licking Ohio. We think we will *try* and be worthy the notice of the Son of a Tory.

We understand that Prince Beck Phillips, English Green Dick, and the Bowery Dog, were appointed a committee by the Mayor com and and all the chief coons of the city, to ascertain and report the-the-the *probable* number of persons in attendance at the great coon State central, Alfred Kelly, Samson Mason, mass meeting, gathering of Montgomery, Clark, Warren and Clinton counties, held in this place on Wednesday, the 14th inst. We have not yet seen their report. We will agree to publish the name of every person that was in attendance, if you will furnish them for us. This is surely fair, and more than you would do for us. Your own names as committee men shall be at the winding up, the *Dog's* most particularly. Report, gentlemen. Report!!

BAND NOTICE.

Any Democrat wishing to subscribe a mite to further the German town Band will please leave their names at the office of P. P. Lowe Esqr., where a paper will be left for that purpose. The attention of the whole democratic family is invited to the above. The band are in want of a few more democratic instruments, wishing to discard some of a coon nature. They pledge themselves to be always at hand at the command of the democratic central committee of this county.

"Do you hear that boys?" no shirking, but walk *up* and put *down* the pewter ink-toms!

We shall soon believe Senator Barnett's sword descended to him from his *fourfathers* is "all in my eye Betty Martin" or like the *Scottlanders* daddy. Bless my soul, what a thing it is to spring from such *very illustrious* ancestors. Hem!

We have been led to believe that His Honor the Mayor, the Common Council and Marshal, have been so very busy electioneering, that they have overlooked the damage done to the pavement of the Market House by the *Hogs* and the two legged mass grunters on the 14th inst.

What has become of "Tuscan of Liberty," of Albany? We send on regularly. The Coon Killer of Memphis Tenn, has not toed the trig! Numbers 11, 12, 13 and 14 have never come to hand. We send two copies regularly. The Coon Skinner is excused but we hope he may soon recover, and be in at the death.

What Scott Long meant, of course, is that basically political cartooning is a symbolic art. The symbols are a shorthand, a convenience, not only for the artist but for the viewer as well. To alter the symbols, concludes cartoonist Don Hesse of the St. Louis *Globe-Democrat*, "would be like changing the basic design of the American Flag, the Statue of Liberty, or Orphan Annie for that matter. Everyone has grown to know them all on sight. Since cartoonists strive for simplicity and for ideas unencumbered with labels, they use this cast of characters and eliminate the need for a program to tell the players one from the other."[30]

"Don't Mind Me—Just Go Right On Talking"

I-24   *Herblock's Mr. Atom, 1947.*

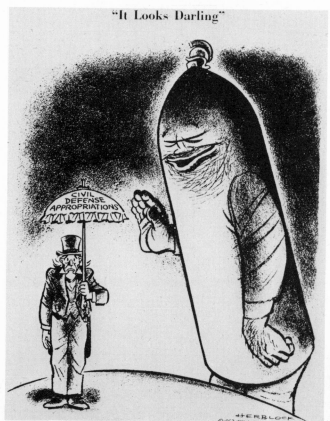

"It Looks Darling"

Yet some symbols do change or disappear over the years. The modern cartoonist, for instance, has dropped Salt River from his repertoire, although it was exceedingly popular in the last century. It meant Defeat, usually of the political variety, and losing candidates (or those whom the cartoonists wished to see lose) were constantly falling into the briny waters. Nast's Rag Baby (for Inflation) had a vogue but ultimately failed to make the grade. The Bear as the symbol for Russia lost its currency after the Bolshevik Revolution of 1917. Columbia proved unequal to Uncle Sam and gradually was replaced as a common cartoon character.

Some symbols are invented to fill a void and have a provable paternity. Nast, the all-time-great symbol maker, is even credited with creating the Santa Claus figure; Kirby created Mr. Dry during the Prohibition era; Daniel R. Fitzpatrick of the St. Louis *Post-Dispatch* was able to give the Swastika a truly menacing meaning in the 1930s; and Herblock brought forth a continuing character called Mr. Atom.

I-25   Mr. Atom, *1954. Herblock kept making this figure more sinister. "I felt a good deal of satisfaction when people used to tell me, with flattering exaggeration, that the Atom character gave them the shivers," reported the cartoonist. "But when I began hearing about 'that cute Mr. Atom you draw,' I gave him longer rest periods."*

But many of the key symbols simply evolved, their origins now lost in the past, with different artists adding embellishments over the years. One such character is Uncle Sam. Before he made an appearance, the United States was represented by Brother Jonathan. There is a persistent story, though adequately discredited by Albert Matthews in 1902, that the model for Jonathan was Governor Jonathan Trumbull of Connecticut. Although Matthews was not able to locate the true origin even after painstaking research, he did conclude that Jonathan was "a mildly derisive epithet" used by the Loyalists during the Revolutionary War for those who espoused the American cause; that when the Americans took it up later in the eighteenth century they used it to designate a country bumpkin; and that it was finally accepted as an appellation for the Americans by the very people whom it was originally meant to ridicule.[31]

Although the name Uncle Sam is generally thought to have come from one Samuel Wilson of Troy, New York, a government meat inspector during the War of 1812, the cartoon model was definitely an evolution of the Brother Jonathan figure, although there is one early lithograph in which Brother Jonathan and Uncle Sam appear together.

In 1959 Allan Nevins wrote, "It is time that the most complicated nation on earth disowned this crude stereotype." He called Uncle Sam "an infantile folk image" and "a mischievous oversimplification." But the eminent historian's advice will go unheeded if for no other reason than—as Rollin Kirby once said—"it would be difficult to manage a daily cartoon" without him.[32]

I-26 *This* Brother Jonathan *was done during the War of 1812 to "inspire our countrymen with confidence in themselves," wrote the artist, Amos Doolittle, "and eradicate any terrors that they may feel as respects the enemy they have to combat." It sold wholesale for seven dollars per hundred when purchased in lots of a hundred.*

BROTHER JONATHAN *Administering a Salutary Cordial to* JOHN BULL.

I-27 *In the first known cartoon of Uncle Sam, 1832, he is shown as a sick man surrounded by quack doctors Thomas Hart Benton, Amos Kendall, Andrew Jackson, and Martin Van Buren.*

UNCLE SAM'S PET PUPS!
Or, Mother BANK'S last refuge.
Sold at ELTON'S, 18 Division-Street, New-York.

I-28 *By 1840 Uncle Sam had just acquired the now-traditional top hat and striped pants. Here he chases Jackson and Van Buren into the "hard cider" barrel held, presumably, by General Harrison.*

LINCOLN'S TWO DIFFICULTIES.

Lis. "WHAT? NO MONEY! NO MEN!"

I-29 *During the Civil War Punch and its chief cartoonist, Sir John Tenniel, helped along the evolution of Uncle Sam by giving him the visage of the bewhiskered Abraham Lincoln.*

I-30 *"The c–a–artoonists," said Mr. Dooley, the barkeep sage, "make Uncle Sam with a hairses ta–el fer phiskers and a fla–ag fer paants." Modifications in Uncle Sam's whiskers were made by both Nast and Keppler until he finally reached maturity in the World War I poster-cartoons of Charles Dana Gibson (right) and James Montgomery Flagg (opposite page).*

His Mother. HERE HE IS, SIR

I-31

NOTICE TO QUIT.

March 4th 1841.

I-32 *Jack Downing, symbolizing the American people, indicates that he is locking Van Buren out of the White House in favor of William Henry Harrison.*

The Log Cabin, an 1840 Whig campaign newspaper published by Horace Greeley, said of "Notice to Quit" that "no man can glance over [it] without feeling a broad smile rippling over, warming, mellowing and illumining his whole countenance."

Just as cartoonists have always had some character or symbol to represent the American *nation*, so, too, has there always been a character to represent the American *people*. In the 1830s and '40s he was called Jack Downing after a fictional Yankee peddler created by humorist Seba Smith.

The present form of the symbol was invented by Frederick Opper at the end of the nineteenth century. Opper's little man was labeled The Common People. He also would be known as John Public, and around 1930 Vaughn Shoemaker, then of the Chicago *Daily News*, gave him a middle initial: John Q. Public.

Although the Democratic Donkey and the Republican Elephant are both often called the inventions of Thomas Nast, he is entitled to credit for only the latter. There have been donkeys around as the symbol of the Democratic

I-33   *The editor of* The Arena *in 1905 called Opper's character "a foolish, cowed, insignificant and contemptible pigmy. . . ." Indeed, Mr. Common People seems like a strange symbol for Americans to choose as their representative.*

I-34   *One of the most amusing variations on the Mr. Common People theme was Taxpayer-in-the-barrel by Will B. Johnstone, who wrote and directed Marx Brothers movies while drawing cartoons for the New York* World-Telegram.

THE MODERN BALAAM AND HIS ASS.

I-35   *The first Democratic Donkey, 1837.*

I-36   *The first Republican Elephant, 1874.*

party or of leading Democratic politicians since the days of Andrew Jackson. But the G.O.P. elephant was born in a *Harper's Weekly* cartoon of November 7, 1874, in which Nast tried to counter a newspaper story that President Grant was planning to break tradition by seeking a third term. The inspiration for the cartoon was a then-recent newspaper hoax known as "The Central Park Menagerie Scare." (The New York *Herald* reported that the animals had escaped from the zoo and were roaming the mid-Manhattan park in search of prey.) Among Nast's rampaging animals was the future symbol of the Republican party. (Nast, a good Republican, pictured the Democratic party not as a donkey, but as a fox!)

A number of attempts have been made to change the party symbols. The Democrats have been represented by a rooster in some southern states. The Republicans have used an eagle on the ballot in Oklahoma, and the Democrats have used the eagle in adjoining New Mexico. But the public has cast its ballot for the Elephant and Donkey, even though they have lost whatever significance they might have originally had.[33]

"Caricatures," wrote Emerson in his *Journal*, "are often the truest history of the times." The graphic caricature or cartoon not only provides a record of the vernacular—the dress and design,

I-37   *Jim Berry, Newspaper Enterprise Association, 1964.*

GETTIN' BACK AT THE CARTOONISTS.

CAPITOL WITH TREE

LABELS LABELS
LABELS LABELS

FREE TRADE SYMBOL

PROTECTION-SYMBOL

ITICAL CHINE

THE PROPERTY ROOM OF THE CLEVER CARTOONIST

fads and foibles—but also represents a stop-action picture of what a group of talented observers feels is noteworthy at a particular moment. Yet a survey of more than two hundred years of American political cartooning is bound to have a built-in bias against drawings that illustrate those events that weigh most lightly on the scales of history. The local is apt to be pushed aside by the national; a comment on a President is likely to take precedent over one on a mayor.

The local cartoon, however, has played a not insignificant role in the annals of cartooning. Thomas Nast, whose campaign against the Tweed ring is a notable example, was an eighteen-year-old, $7-a-week artist on

I-38 *Frederick Richardson, Chicago* Daily News, *1899. Although he had been a well-known political cartoonist for fifteen years, Richardson is today best remembered for his children's book illustrations. Another artist who also found that it was a short leap from politics to fantasy was Palmer Cox, creator of* The Brownies.

Frank Leslie's Illustrated Newspaper when that journal, partly through its art work, forced a clean-up of the "swill milk" business, one of the vilest practices in New York City history.

John Chase, who draws political cartoons for WDSU-TV in New Orleans, has written, "The American cartoonist in the 1960's has a considerable following in his own neighborhood, and his first responsibility is to be routinely effective and provocative to this regional readership." In this era of syndication not all of Chase's colleagues would agree with this definition of a cartoonist's first duty. Nonetheless, a number of current practitioners have built solid reputations primarily on their handling of local events. Any politically saavy Baltimorean can tell at a glance the relative strengths of all the city's "bosslets" from the detailed cartoons that the *Sun's* Richard Q. Yardley draws of the

I-39 *Three New York City aldermen whitewash a diseased cow whose tail has rotted off as a result of having been fed refuse from a distillery, 1858.*

CAMPAIGNING WITH BATHHOUSE JOHN

COURIER FROM THE FRONT — *"They've routed the 'Old Guard,' General!"*

THIRTY-FIRST YEAR   SAN FRANCISCO, CAL., DECEMBER 1, 1906.   VOL. LVI, NO. 22

"WE ARE PURE AND HIGH MINDED PATRIOTS PERSECUTED BY OUR POLITICAL ENEMIES!"

I-40   *(above left)* John T. McCutcheon frequently noted the turn-of-the-century antics of "Bathhouse John" Coughlin and Michael (Hinky-Dink) Kenna, the notorious alderman from Chicago's first ward. "Bathhouse John" earned his nickname honestly as a rubber in a Turkish bath. He once told Carter Henry Harrison that he had been reelected mayor "because of the public satisfaction with the well-known honesty that has caricatured your every administration!"

I-41   *(above right)* The Wasp of San Francisco lost some of its sting after Ambrose Bierce left as editor, but in 1906 it still mustered a campaign against Boss Abe Ruef (right) and his puppet mayor, "Handsome Gene" Schmitz, a violinist, who extracted payoffs from saloons, houses of prostitution, and other business establishments.

AFTER ONE HUNDRED FIFTY-NINE YEARS

I-42   *Year after year the* Washington Star's *Clifford K. Berryman reminded Congress of his city's voteless status. This cartoon appeared in 1934.*

"b'hoys." And Francis Dahl has become such an institution to readers of the Boston *Herald Traveler* that Ogden Nash has written a poem about his merits that begins:

I sing this tome of Francis Dahl's,
Whose pencil never spits or snahls,
Who in the kindliest of humors
Surveyeth Boston's beans and
    bloomers . . .[34]

While many American cartoonists have chosen to adopt an Olympian detachment toward the events they describe, the best practitioners since the late nineteenth century generally have not been satisfied to remain observers; they have sought to shape events rather than merely record them. Walt Kelly has compared their proper function to that of the watchdog. "It is the duty of the watchdog to growl warnings, to bark, to surmise that every strange footfall is that of a cat, to worry about birds, and to suspect unknown insects."[35] How successful have the cartoonists been as participants? And how can such success be measured? On rare occasions the results are dramatic and irrefutable, such as the downfall of Boss Tweed. But most often the best that can be said is that the cartoonists have been an influence, albeit one of many. Ulysses Grant is quoted as having said in 1868, "Two things elected me: the sword of Sheridan and the pencil of Thomas Nast." Grover Cleveland

Examples of two effective local series directed against crime syndicates.

I-43 *D. R. Fitzpatrick's "Rat Alley" in the St. Louis* Post–Dispatch.

I-44 *Jacob Burck's "Hood Row" in the Chicago* Sun–Times.

46

is reported to have credited *Puck*'s cartoons with having made him President. William McKinley is supposed to have claimed that *Judge*'s artists were responsible for his election.[36] But the three Presidents might not have been the best judges of their own successes; moreover, Cleveland was known to be generous in distributing credit. (He also claimed his first victory was the result of Pulitzer's support).[37]

Another indicator of the influence of cartoons—or perhaps just of their sting —has been the anguished yelps of those ridiculed. "A good caricature," said a nineteenth-century artist, "is only fully appreciated by those who have been its victims."

One politician who felt himself particularly discriminated against by the cartoonists was Governor Samuel Pennypacker of Pennsylvania. By 1903 he had reached the end of his patience and announced to the state legislature, "In England a century ago the [cartoonist] offender would have been drawn and quartered and his head stuck upon a pole without the gates. In America today this is the kind of arrogance which 'goeth before a fall.' "[38]

The 1899 California legislature, whose members had felt the wrath of San Francisco cartoonists, outlawed any caricatures that reflected on a person's character and the publication of any portrait without the consent of the subjects. The laws produced laughter rather than compliance and were eventually repealed.[39] Similar attempts to pass anti-cartoon legislation were made in New York (1897), Indiana (1913), and Alabama (1915).

MESSRS. KLAW AND ERLANGER PRESENT "MR. BLUEBEARD," LATE OF THE IROQUOIS THEATRE.

I-45 *This* Life *cartoon appeared three weeks after the tragic Iroquois Theatre fire in Chicago, 1904. Messrs. Klaw and Erlanger, alleging that they had been libeled, sued the magazine for $100,000, but* Life *won the case by proving that the drawing accurately represented the condition of the theatre's exits at the time of the fire.*

"It may well be doubted whether ever before in the history of American politics such an event (as my nomination) has occurred."—FROM JUDGE PENNYPACKER'S RECENT SPEECH AT THE ACADEMY OF MUSIC.

I-46 *In 1902 Charles Nelan of the Philadelphia* North American *drew a series in which Governor Pennypacker was cast as a parrot, a bird the political leader felt was not in keeping with his dignity. His response was to get a friendly legislator to introduce a bill to prohibit "the depicting of men . . . as birds or animals."*

I-47 *This prompted cartoonist Walt McDougall, also of the Philadelphia* North American, *to draw the state's top officials as such inhuman objects as oaks and squashes. The governor (a beet), according to the artist, "thereafter refused to acknowledge my courteous salute . . . on the street."*

"They Never Liked Cartoons."

I-48 *When Thomas Platt had an anti-cartoon bill presented to the New York legislature in 1897, cartoonist Homer Davenport compared him to "Boss" Tweed (drawn in the Nast manner).*

I-49 *Then, after the bill was killed, Davenport drew another cartoon entitled, "There are some who laugh and others who weep," in which he pictured himself laughing while Platt and Tweed shed tears.*

Non Votis, &c.

II-1   *Benjamin Franklin, 1747.*

II

Copper Engraving
and Woodcut
1747-1828

A wagon is stuck in the mud and its driver prays to be pulled out of his predicament by mighty Hercules (seen perched on a cloud). The Latin caption says, in effect, "God helps those who help themselves." The hackneyed idea and crude design hardly deserve attention—except that this is the first known American political cartoon.

"Non Votis" (or "The Waggoner and Hercules") was drawn by Benjamin Franklin in 1747 to illustrate his pamphlet *Plain Truth,* in which the Philadelphia printer urged militant Pennsylvanians to prepare for defense even though they would be defending the noncombatant Quakers. He wrote, "Till of late I could scarce believe the story of him who refused to pump in a sinking ship because one on board whom he hated would be saved by it as well as himself." The pamphlet, Franklin later said in his *Autobiography,* "had a sudden and surprising effect," helping to raise a militia of 10,000 volunteers.[1]

It has been called "a curious irony" that Franklin, the first American political cartoonist, should also have been the first public figure in America to have been ridiculed by cartoons. Indeed, half of the eight cartoons that art historian William Murrell attributes to this period have Franklin as their foil.

II-2 *In this detail from a 1764 engraving, the Devil whispers in Franklin's ear, "Thee shall be my agent Ben for all my realms." The Devil was a constantly recurring figure in American political cartoons until the mid-nineteenth century.*

Franklin, the seventeenth child of a Boston tallow chandler, had started his career as an apprentice printer at the age of twelve. He later ran away to Philadelphia and eventually opened his own printing establishment. As a printer, it was not unusual for him to become involved in such allied pursuits as writing, publishing, and compiling the highly lucrative *Poor Richard's* almanacs. Nor was it surprising that as Franklin grew well-to-do he devoted more of his time to scientific experiments and public affairs. A year after he drew America's first political cartoon, the by-then prosperous printer retired from trade.

In 1754, Franklin, the inspired amateur, made one of the great "lucky hits" (as Allan Nevins and Frank Weitenkampf called it). That year he represented Pennsylvania at the Albany Congress, where he proposed a "Plan of Union" for the colonies. In its support he drew the famous serpent divided into eight parts with the legend, "Join or Die." The cartoon was based on the popular superstition that a snake that had been severed would come back to life if the pieces were put together before sunset.[2] It appeared in the *Pennsylvania Gazette* of May 9, the first cartoon to be published in an American newspaper, and within a month had been reprinted by virtually every newspaper on the continent. The serpent device, moreover, was to have three lives. It was dusted off at the time of the Stamp Act crisis in 1765 and again when the colonies prepared to revolt in 1774.

Having the American revolutionaries depict their cause as a dissected snake was thought a good joke by one loyalist editor, James Rivington, who published this verse in his *New York Gazeteer*:

Ye sons of Sedition, how comes it to pass
That America's typed by a snake—in the grass?
Don't you think 'tis a scandalous, saucy reflection
That merits the soundest, severest correction?
New England's the head, too— New England's abused
For the Head of the Serpent we know should be bruised.

II-3　*Franklin's original snake, 1754.*

JOIN, or DIE.

Yet the "Sons of Liberty" would have the last laugh. For when Cornwallis surrendered, the serpent made still another appearance: an English cartoon by Gillray showed the defeated British camp completely encircled by a huge rattlesnake.[3]

Publisher Isaiah Thomas' decision in 1774 to add the "Join or Die" serpent to the masthead of his *Massachusetts Spy* unwittingly united the names of two American patriots—Benjamin Franklin, who had invented the design, and Paul Revere, its engraver. The latter was a little-known figure until 1860, when Longfellow composed the poem that began: "Listen, my children, and you shall hear/Of the midnight ride of Paul Revere. . . ." Revere's ride, of course, was to alert the countryside that the British were preparing to march on Concord.[4]

By profession Revere was a silversmith, a trade whose prospects varied in direct relation to the state of the economy. When times were good, people could afford the luxuries that Revere made and sold; when times were bad, they were especially bad for artisan Revere. So it was that during recessions he applied his skill to turning out a less-expensive product—engravings that could be sold individually as broadsides for a few pennies.

Revere's best known engraving was a scene of the grandiloquently named "Boston Massacre," March 5, 1770. A mob had attacked some British troops,

II-4   *The snake at the time of the Stamp Act crisis, 1765.*

II-5   *Paul Revere's engraving of the snake on the eve of the Revolution, 1774. The addition of Georgia (the tail) gave it a ninth section.*

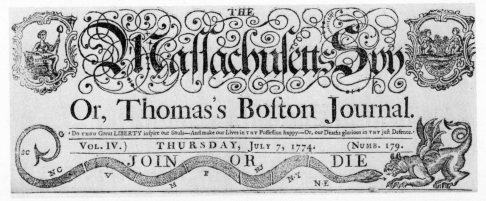

II-6   *Paul Revere's engraving of the Boston Massacre, 1770, was hand-colored for greater vividness.*

and when the smoke had cleared four Americans were dead. The Revere engraving, although masquerading as a realistic picture of the event, was really a political cartoon meant as propaganda for the anti-British element. Over the British Custom House, Revere placed a sign "Butcher's Hall" (upper right). Moreover, Revere, who had made a very accurate pen-and-ink diagram of the "Massacre," was well aware that the shootings did not happen in the wanton fashion shown in his broadside. (Strangely, too, Revere's engraving changed the race of one of the fallen Americans, Crispus Attucks, a towering Negro.) The cartoon apparently was considered so inflammatory that when the soldiers were brought to trial one of their lawyers sternly warned the jurors against being biased by prints that add "wings to fancy."[5]

Three days after Revere's Boston Massacre engraving went on sale he received the following letter from John Singleton Copley's stepbrother, artist Henry Pelham:

THURSDAY MORN[IN]G, BOSTON, MARCH 29, 1770.

SIR,

When I heard that you were cutting a plate of the late Murder, I thought it impossible as I knew you was not capable of doing it unless you copied it from mine and as I thought I had entrusted it in the hands of a person who had more regard to the dictates of Honour and Justice than to take the undue advantage you have done of the confidence and Trust I reposed in you. But I find I was mistaken and after being at the great Trouble and Expense of making a design paying for paper, printing &c. find myself in the most ungenerous Manner deprived not only of any proposed Advantage but even of the expense I have been at, as truly as if you had plundered me on the highway. If you are insensible of the Dishonour you have brought on yourself by this Act, the World will not be so. However, I leave you to reflect upon and consider of one of the most dishonourable Actions you could well be guilty of.

H. PELHAM

Pelham's charge was correct. Revere was an engraver (by virtue of his training as a silversmith) and had no artistic ability or pretension. No record exists of his having made a reply to Pelham. At best, it can be said that he "borrowed" Pelham's work out of patriotic impulse. (The anti-British additions to the plate were his; Pelham was to become a Tory.) But it is more likely that Revere simply was following the eighteenth-century engravers' custom of copying anything they wished, without credit or acknowledgment. In England the "Hogarth Act" of 1735 protected an engraver for fourteen years against piracy of his print. But in the faraway American colonies engravers were less scrupulous and it was seldom considered illegal or improper to copy another man's work.

Finis Coronat Opus.

Revere added more fuel to the debate over the Boston Massacre by engraving a cut of four coffins, each with the initials of one of the Americans killed by the British troops on March 5. This was just the beginning of the macabre symbolism that was to be the most prominent feature of American cartoons during the Colonial period and that

II-7, II-8 *A 1768 Revere cartoon (below) and the 1765 English print on which it was modeled.*

The main change made by the Boston silversmith was to increase to seventeen

the number of men being pushed into Hell. This represented the members of the Massachusetts House of Representatives who voted in favor of rescinding a "circulatory letter" that criticized Parliament for levying taxes on the colonies. Ironically, the patriotic poem about the "brave rescinders," which appeared beneath Revere's engraving, was by Dr. Benjamin Church, who was to be convicted of being a traitor to the Revolutionary cause.

The 29th Regiment have already left us, and the 14th Regiment are following them, so that we expect the Town will foon be clear of all the Troops. The Wifdom and true Policy of his Majefty's Council and Col. Dalrymple the Commander appear in this Meafure. Two Regiments in the midft of this populous City; and the Inhabitants juftly incenfed: Thofe of the neighbouring Towns actually under Arms upon the firft Report of the Maffacre, and the Signal only wanting to bring in a few Hours to the Gates of this City many Thoufands of our brave Brethren in the Country, deeply affected with our Diftreffes, and to whom we are greatly obliged on this Occafion—No one knows where this would have ended, and what important Confequences even to the whole Britifh Empire might have followed, which our Moderation & Loyalty upon fo trying an Occafion, and our Faith in the Commander's Affurances have happily prevented.

Laft Thurfday, agreeable to a general Requeft of the Inhabitants, and by the Confent of Parents and Friends, were carried to their *Grave* in Succeffion, the Bodies of *Samuel Gray, Samuel Maverick, James Caldwell,* and *Crifpus Attucks,* the unhappy Victims who fell in the bloody Maffacre of the Monday Evening preceeding!

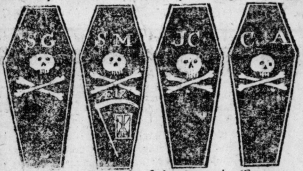

On this Occafion moft of the Shops in Town were fhut, all the Bells were ordered to toll a folemn Peal, as were alfo thofe in the neighboring Towns of Charleftown Roxbury, &c. The Proceffion began to move between the Hours of 4 and 5 in the Afternoon; two of the unfortunate Sufferers, viz. Meff. *James Caldwell* and *Crifpus Attucks,* who were Strangers, borne from Faneuil-Hall, attended by a numerous Train of Perfons of all Ranks; and the other two, viz. Mr. *Samuel Gray,* from the Houfe of Mr. *Benjamin Gray,* (his Brother) on the North-fide the Exchange, and Mr. *Maverick,* from the Houfe of his diftreffed Mother Mrs. *Mary Maverick,* in Union-Street, each followed by their refpective Relations and Friends: The feveral Hearfes forming a Junction in King-Street, the Theatre of that inhuman Tragedy! proceeded from thence thro' the Main-Street, lengthened by an immenfe Concourfe of People, fo numerous as to be obliged to follow in Ranks of fix, and brought up by a long Train of Carriages belonging to the principal Gentry of the Town. The Bodies were depofited in one Vault in the middle Burying-ground: The aggravated Circumftances of their Death, the Diftrefs and Sorrow vifible in every Countenance, together with the peculiar Solemnity with which the whole Funeral was conducted, furpafs Defcription.

A military watch has been kept every night at the

II-9 *Revere added a fifth coffin when another American died as a result of the Boston Massacre. The* Gazette *paid him six shillings for the engravings.*

reached its height on October 31, 1765, the day before the notorious Stamp Act was to take effect. On that date six newspapers, from South Carolina to New Hampshire, went into mourning by encasing their front pages with black borders. (Newspapers were on the list of articles to be taxed.) By far the most lugubrious of the papers was the *Pennsylvania Journal,* published by William Bradford, third-generation scion of America's first great newspaper dynasty.[6]

In the Stamp Act controversy, the colonies were not without support from the English cartoonists. In fact, even during the early stages of the Revolutionary War, London-made engravings and mezzotints were sympathetic to the Americans. It was not until the French entered the war that the English cartoonists rallied to the support of their King.

During the Colonial period and the early years of the Republic the appearance of a political cartoon in America was still an event of considerable rarity. Frank Weitenkampf counted only 78 political caricatures issued before 1828, while cartoons in newspapers and magazines appeared even less frequently.[7] Newsprint was extremely expensive and so scarce that at times readers were urgently requested to save rags for the paper mills. Publishers had little means to pay for the cartoons that had to be so laboriously engraved on copper or cut into wood.[8] Thus cartoons were used primarily to illustrate major events and usually dealt with general principles. It was not unknown for a drawing to appear a second or third time with a different caption. (Even as late as the Civil War it was possible to find a Confederate magazine using a picture of a half-naked Hindu labeled "Abraham Lincoln" and the next month using the same cut—this time labeled "Horace Greeley.")

II-10 *Bradford's celebrated "Tombstone Number" complete with funeral urns and a skull-and-crossbones stamp.*

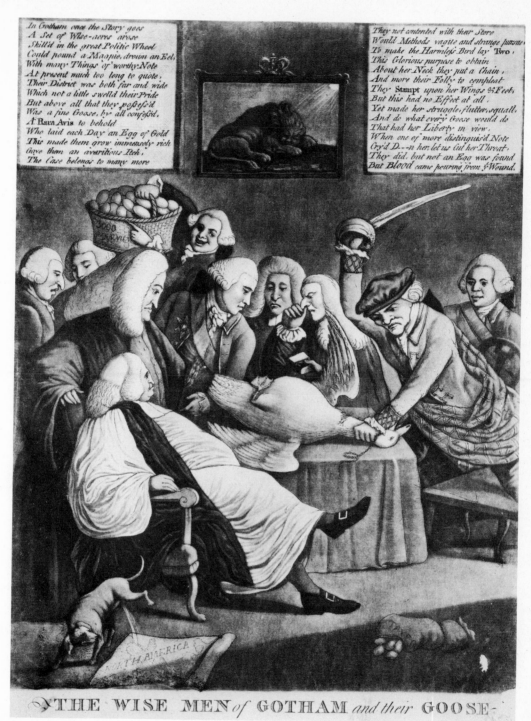

In Gotham once the Story goes
A Set of Wise-acres arose
Skill'd in the great Politic Wheel
Could pound a Maapie, drown an Eel,
With many Things of worthy Note
At present much too long to quote,
Their District was both far and wide
Which not a little swell'd their Pride
But above all that they poss'ss'd
Was a fine Goose, by all confess'd,
A Rara Avis to behold
Who laid each Day an Egg of Gold
This made them grow immensely rich
Gave them an avaritious Itch,
The Case belongs to many more

They not contented with their Store
Would Methods vague and strange pursue
To make the Harmless Bird lay Two
This Glorious purpose to obtain
About her Neck they put a Chain,
And more their Folly to compleat
They Stampt upon her Wings & Feet,
But this had no Effect at all
Yet made her struggle, flutter, squall,
And do what every Goose would do
That had her Liberty in view.
When one of more distinguish'd Note
Cry'd D---n her, let us Cut her Throat,
They did, but not an Egg was found
But Blood came pouring from ye Wound.

THE WISE MEN of GOTHAM and their GOOSE-

II-11   *In this mezzotint, published in London ten months after the Battle of Lexington and Concord, the artist shows King George and his cabinet killing the goose that laid the golden egg.*

The Gerry-mander.

☞ *A new species of Monster, which appeared in Essex South District in January last.*

II-12

Shortly after George Washington's inauguration in 1789, John Armstrong wrote General Gates from New York, "All the world here are busy in collecting flowers and sweets of every kind to amuse and delight the President. . . . Yet in the midst of this admiration there are skeptics who doubt its propriety, and wits who amuse themselves at its extravagance. The first will grumble and the last will laugh, and the President should be prepared to meet the attacks of both with firmness and good nature. A caricature has already appeared, called 'The Entry,' full of very disloyal and profane allusions."[9]

No copy of this print exists, but it is known to have shown Washington riding on a donkey, led by his aide, David Humphreys. The accompanying couplet read: "The glorious time has come to pass/When David shall conduct an ass." Washington, always sensitive to criticism, would not be the last President to discover for himself that the cartooning fraternity respected neither rank nor previous achievement.

Indeed Washington was treated gently compared to Jefferson. Today it is almost impossible to find a pro-Jefferson cartoon. A typical example shows the third President kneeling at the "Altar of Gallic Despotism," about to throw the Constitution into the flames.[10]

Possibly the best—certainly the most famous—of the early nineteenth-century cartoons was for more than a hun-dred years attributed to Gilbert Stuart. The story went that the famous artist, visiting the office of *Massachusetts Centinel* editor Benjamin Russell in 1812, observed a map of the newly created Essex County senatorial district. With a few strokes of his pencil, Stuart added a head, wing, and claws to the map. "That will do for a salamander," he commented. "Salamander? Better call it Gerrymander," said Russell, giving credit for the misshapen district to Governor Elbridge Gerry.[11] Unfortunately for this pleasant tale, the cartoon was drawn by Elkanah Tisdale. (Tisdale's "Gerrymander" was not the first American cartoon to enrich the language. Pennsylvania became known as "the keystone state" because of an eighteenth-century print that gave it the central position in the arc of the federal Union.)[12]

At least four American-born artists —Tisdale, James Akin (the wit who decorated chamber pots with a caricature of his publisher), Amos Doolittle, and Dr. Alexander Anderson—were doing some interesting work during the first quarter of the nineteenth century. Yet it remained for a Scotsman, William Charles, to become the United States' first widely acclaimed political cartoonist.

William Charles of Edinburgh unwillingly left his native isle about 1806. His escape to America was the direct result of his always frisky graver, for

II-13, II-14 *Charles's 1813 cartoon on George III (below) bore a striking resemblance to Gillray's caricature of Napoleon, 1806.*

he was then in difficulty with the ecclesiastics over a print that reflected on their morals. According to Murrell, the offensive engraving probably was "A Fallen Pillar of the Kirk," in which a clergyman bounces a bare-bosomed young woman on his knee, while exclaiming, "Oh Lord, what good things dost thou provide for us men!"[13]

Almost all of Charles's two or three dozen cartoons dealt with the War of 1812, an encounter that gave him ample opportunity to get even with the English. He also showed his contempt —or admiration—for the land of his birth by borrowing heavily and unblushingly from Gillray and Rowlandson. But he was not without a certain originality that was notable for its earthy humor, a quality that was in marked contrast with his other specialty—designing children's books.

II-15, II-16   *A Charles woman (right) was not unlike one drawn by Rowlandson.*

Johnny wont you take some more
Perry! I did not think it was
composed of such strong Ingredients
— Her up — I wish I had not tried
its strength. I I I am quite
over powerd by it —

Oh 'Perry!!! Curse that Perry! It has
Griped me enough already — Such a revolution
in my guts — One disaster after another
I have not half recovered of the Bloody nose
I got at the Boxing Match!

Queen Charlotte and Johnny Bull Get their dose of Perry

II-17 William Charles's robust humor was boldest when he pictured King George on a commode in this comment on Oliver Hazard Perry's victory over Barclay, which secured control of Lake Erie for the Americans.

The artist's Rabelaisian touches included Queen Charlotte offering her husband some "Perry," the name for a drink made from pear juice, "apt to produce uncomfortable digestive phenomena," in the words of one author. Beneath the print was the verse: "On Erie's wave, while Barclay brave/With Charlotte *making merry,/He chanced to take the belly-ache/We drenched him so with Perry."*

Charlotte *was one of the defeated British ships, and the bawdy pun on the Queen's name was not accidental.*

II-18 This anti-Tammany cartoon of Tisdale's, 1808, was commissioned by John Huggins, a New York barber, known for his witty advertisements.

Infant Liberty nursed by Mother Mob.

SOCIAL QUALITIES OF OUR CANDIDATE.

II-19 *Franklin Pierce, 1852.*

II-20 *Daniel Webster, 1852.*

Politicians also were apt to be shown in various compromising positions, notably as drunkards, possibly because libel laws were not serious obstacles to what could appear in print.

II-21 *Ulysses S. Grant, 1872.*

Daniel in the Lion's Den.

"THE FISH QUESTION WILL BE SETTLED, AS THE BULWER TREATY WAS, WITH THE BRITISH MINISTER OVER A BOTTLE OF BRANDY."—[*Democratic Review.*]

Nicholas Biddle holds the head of "Mother Bank"; doctors Clay, Calhoun, and Webster consult; while President Jackson and that everyman, "Major Downing," peer through the window, 1833.

Charles was not alone in introducing a bit of scatological humor into his cartoons. A shocked Clifford Berryman wrote in 1926: ". . . our respectable ancestors had not the least notion of what we call decency."[14]

Certainly the eighteenth- and early nineteenth-century cartoonists had no qualms about picturing female breasts. Paul Revere in 1774 even drew America as a naked woman, her hands and legs held fast by bewigged gentlemen, while tea is being poured down her throat.

In one of the few extant cartoons of George Washington, a dog is shown cocking his leg over an anti-Administration newspaper.

Yet there was an interesting dichotomy between what could be drawn and what could be written. In one 1833 cartoon, "Mother U.S. Bank" is seen vomiting the government's funds, while Nicholas Biddle says, "D – – n that Doctor Jackson . . ." Another print of the Jacksonian era has the salty President saying, "What a h – – l of a hand old Harrison's got." The cartoonists obviously felt that even such mild epithets as "damn" and "hell" were too offensive to be spelled out, illustrating again how each age sets its own standards of decency.

Although Ulysses S. Grant repeatedly would be pictured in a tipsy condition during the 1872 election, by the Reconstruction period the reading (or looking) public was adopting new standards of "refinement." *The Nation* magazine wrote in 1866 of how Gillray's works "would not now be tolerated by good society, and hardly relished by the frequenters of gin-palaces and beershops."[15]

For political cartoons to have mass appeal required two developments: a process that could cut the cost of production and a subject colorful enough to inspire broad interest and controversy. The election of 1828 produced both —lithography and Andrew Jackson.

To some Jackson was the savior, the people's friend, a giant who fought their battles against the British and the vested interests; to others he was a tyrant, "King Andrew the first." But everyone felt strongly about him—one way or the other—and everything he did was tumultous.

II-23

KING ANDREW THE FIRST.

II-24   *Josiah Quincy, 1813.*

Having fought a Revolutionary War to end rule by royalty, the figure of King, Czar, or Emperor as a symbol of opprobrium would be a steady theme running through the history of the nation's political cartoons.

II-26   *Thomas B. Reed, 1894.*

II-25   *Andrew Johnson (left) and William Seward, 1866.*

II-27 *Peggy Eaton, the wife of Jackson's Secretary of War, had a dubious background and was snubbed by the other Cabinet wives. The chivalrous President's intercession in her behalf led to the resignation of his Cabinet. Edward Williams Clay's comment on Martin Van Buren as the third rat from the left prompted his son to reply, when asked when his father would be returning to New York: "When the President takes off his foot." Mrs. Trollope called this "the only tolerable" cartoon she saw during her travels in America.*

The Rats leaving a Falling House.

II-28 *Henry Clay's successful effort to have the Senate censure Jackson during the President's war on the Bank of the United States inspired this cartoon by David Claypoole Johnston, 1834.*

These two spirited cartoons were highly unusual for the period. At a time when *cartoonists believed that their work improved in direct proportion to the number of characters and balloons they could squeeze into their drawings, Johnston and Clay kept their figures and captions to a minimum.*

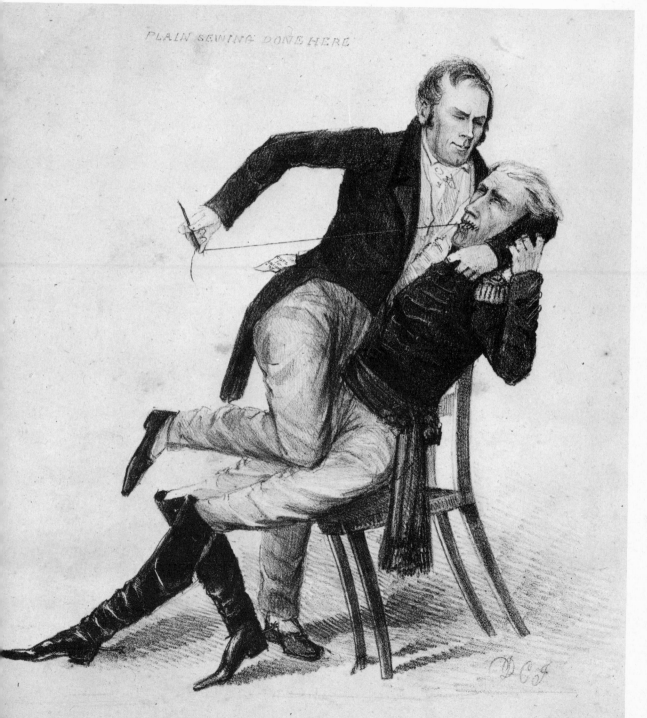

SYMPTOMS OF A LOCKED JAW

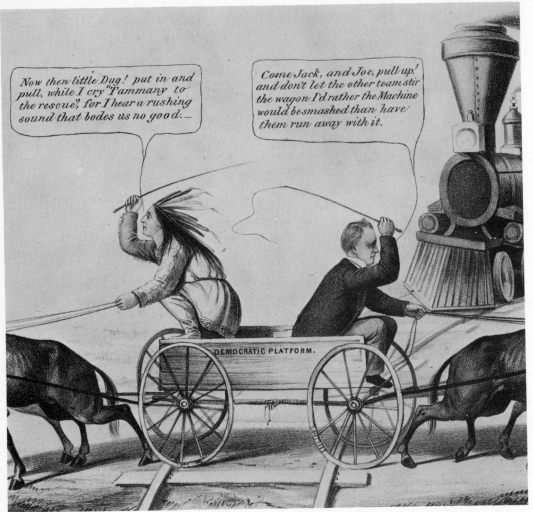

Detail from III-1 *"Progressive Democracy—Prospect of a Smash Up," Currier & Ives, 1860.*

III

Lithography and Early Magazines 1828-65

Lithography is based on a principle well known to every housewife: grease and water do not mix.

The artist draws directly on a limestone slab with a wax crayon. After the stone has been bathed in a mixture of water and gum arabic, an oil-based ink can be absorbed by the areas that have been covered by the wax, which has a high fat content, but the ink is repelled by the waxfree areas where there is no chemical affinity. Thus the moistened stone can deliver a faithful image to a sheet of paper.

This process—much simpler than engraving or woodcut—was invented about 1795 by a Bavarian, Alois Senefelder, and introduced in America by Bass Otis in the *Analectic Magazine* of July, 1819. The first lithographed political cartoon did not appear until 1829, however, when an anonymous artist, probably an amateur, commented on the then-recent Presidential election by drawing a map of the United States with an alligator, representing the Jacksonian party, stretched across the western states, and a tortoise, for the party of John Quincy Adams, spread over the country's eastern half.

The most prolific publisher of political lithographs in the years between 1831 and 1849 was Henry R. Robinson, New York, of whom almost nothing is known. He drew many of his own designs and also employed several other capable artists, notably Edward Williams Clay and Napoleon Sarony. But by far the most famous lithographic firm was that of Currier & Ives. Nathaniel Currier, founder of the business in 1835, and James Merritt Ives, whom he hired as a bookkeeper in 1852 and made his partner five years later, turned out an estimated 10 million copies of nearly 7000 different subjects —great fires, railroads, clipper ships, Indians, sporting events, and more than eighty political cartoons.[1]

Although these cartoons sometimes displayed a good sense of composition, the figures were stiff and spiritless. From their mouths issued huge balloon-like loops of text, a method of storytelling by then abandoned in Europe, which reminded later writers of "a grotesque . . . soap-bubble party on a large scale" and "the cowboys of a Wild West show, all engaged in a vain attempt to lasso and pull in their own idle words."[2]

Whatever humor can be found in these political lithographs came from the incongruous and ridiculous situations in which the artists placed public men, rather than from any exaggeration or distortion of the subjects' features. The portraiture of the Currier & Ives artists was so exact that they must have worked directly from daguerro-types or photographs.

Currier & Ives designs were often the product of several hands. One artist might draw the figures and another the background. But "Progressive Democracy—Prospect of a Smash Up" and many of the other political prints, although unsigned, have been identified as the work of Louis Maurer, a German who came to the United States in 1851 and died eighty-one years later in his one hundred and first year. Other artists who were hired by the firm on a free-lance basis included Thomas Worth, John Cameron, and Ben Day (more famous as the inventor of a process for introducing textures and shading line cuts.)

The nonpolitical lithographs were vividly colored by hand, but the political cartoons went out in black and white. They probably were sold to party headquarters at bulk rates, although they could also be purchased individually at prices ranging from five to twenty-five cents. Some had exceedingly large printings—50,000 for "The Ir-

III-1 *In this comment on the 1860 split in the Democratic party (with the Tammany Indian pictured as holding the reins of the northern ticket), the artist uses a technique of hanging human heads in front of animal ears, which is generally associated with seventeenth-century cartooning and is rarely seen in this* *period. The face of Lincoln in all the 1860 Currier & Ives cartoons was taken from Mathew Brady's Cooper Union photograph, and later when the Republican candidate began to grow a beard the lithographer's stones were given the appropriate touch-ups.*

Herschel V. Johnson   Stephen A. Douglas   James Buchanan   Abraham Lincoln   Hannibal Hamlin

John C. Breckinridge

Joseph Lane

PROGRESSIVE DEMOCRACY_PROSPECT OF A SMASH UP.

repressible Conflict," a mildly satirical picture of the Republicans in 1860, possibly drawn by Cameron; and 100,000 for Frank Beard's "Why Don't You Take It?" (1860), in which General Winfield Scott as a ferocious bulldog is guarding a rib of "prize beef" (Washington, D.C.) from Jefferson Davis, who appears as a slinking greyhound.[3] Clearly company policy was business above politics as Mr. Currier and Mr. Ives turned out cartoons for all sides at the same time.

Moreover, in periods when feelings ran high, artistic pride gave way to commercial prudence and the firm left its name off the prints or signed them with the pseudonym "Peter Smith."

Pictorially and textually the prints continued to rely heavily on the pun, a practice, apparently, that was not limited to cartoonists. A *Vanity Fair* author in 1860, noting the reliance of so many early American comics on this form of humor, wrote: "I would restrict the al-

STORMING THE CASTLE

III-2 *A pro-Lincoln lithograph by Currier & Ives, 1860. The Republican candidate wears an oilskin cape, used by the marchers of his "Wide Awake" clubs to protect their clothes from the dripping of the kerosene torches they carried. As usual, Lincoln's fence rail—the symbol of his humble beginnings—is present.*

THE REPUBLICAN PARTY GOING TO THE RIGHT HOUSE.

III-3 *An anti-Lincoln lithograph by Currier & Ives, 1860. Although Louis Maurer, who drew both cartoons, voted for Lincoln, his comment on the "strange" elements which attached themselves to the new Republican party is far more stinging.*

lowance of a punster in good health to 80 or 90 a day, certainly not more than a hundred. I frequently make 6 or 700 before dinner, but then everybody has not my constitution."[4]

Many of the puns, unfortunately, were no more inspired than plays on people's names. This puerility was one of the less majestic contributions to American cartooning made by Great Britain, where, in the eighteenth century, artists were content to represent

III-4   *Quaker George* Fox, *1764.*

III-5   *Confederate Robert* Toombs, *1861.*

"HARK FROM THE *TOOMBS* A DOLEFUL CRY."

III-6   *Former Secretary of State Hamilton* Fish, *1880.*

MORE FISH THAN HE CAN LAND.

III-7   *War Secretary Elihu* Root, *1899.*

"THE MAN WITH THE HOE"

Lord Bute as a pair of boots or Lord North as Boreas, the north wind. Regrettably, American cartoonists became deeply attached to this habit, thus making public service a little more trying for men like Matthew Lyon, Thurlow Weed, and John Bell.

Probably the politician with the most punnable surname was Lewis Cass, whose long career included service as Governor of Michigan Territory, Secretary of War, Secretary of State, U.S. Senator, and Presidential candidate.

The Michigander's last name, cartoonists would be constantly reminding him, rhymed with both *gas* and *ass*.

About as predictable as the cartoonists' puns were the sports motifs that they dusted off every fourth year. Any Presidential election from 1832 to 1864 was sure to be presented as a horse or foot race, a boxing match, a game of brag (an early version of poker), pool or bagatelle, a cock fight, hunting, fishing, a bull fight, or (by 1860) a baseball game.

III-8

A WAR PRESIDENT.

PROGRESSIVE DEMOCRACY.

III-9

A CASS-US OMMISSUS.

III-10

BROTHER, BEWARE.

We hope that our beloved brother Cass will take care of writing letters. Take the first letter from him, and an abominable thing is left, which wouldn't be right. He should C to it at once. This first letter is the rock upon which many a political aspirant has split. Take care of C therefore, and we will take care of U. An examination of the cut below, will show what he will be, when they get the first letter from him.

C-ASS.

III-11   *A boxing match between Van Buren and Harrison, 1836.*

III-12   *Clay and Polk in a cockfight, 1844.*

III-13   *Calhoun, Cass, Clay, Taylor, Buchanan, and Polk at cards, 1848.*

III-14 *A foot race between Webster, Scott, and Pierce, 1852.*

III-15 *Baseball players Bell, Douglas, Breckinridge, and Lincoln, 1860.*

III-16 *Lincoln and McClellan at the bagatelle table, 1864.*

III-17 *Daumier's "Caricature Wielding Her Lash," 1838. Balzac thought the artist had "Michelangelo in his blood"* and *Louis Philippe thought his cartoons were irreverent enough to merit a five-month imprisonment in 1832.*

While cartoonists on the west side of the Atlantic were experiencing a spiritual and artistic near-bankruptcy, their counterparts in France were toppling a throne. As Thackeray wrote, the struggle was between "half a dozen poor artists on the one side and His Majesty Louis Philippe, his august family, and the numberless policemen and supporters of the monarchy on the other. . . ." In 1830 Charles Philipon had started a Paris humor magazine, *La Caricature,* and two years later he added a daily, *Le Charivari,* whose artists, led by Honoré Daumier, were one of the Re-publicans' more effective weapon in their struggle against the king.

It was Philipon's idea to transform Louis Philippe's features into the *poire.* In cartoon after cartoon the pear-shaped monarch was made an object of ridicule to his subjects. For this offense Philipon was put on trial and in his own defense he drew a large Burgundy pear, which he converted in a few strokes to a likeness of the King. "Can I help it if His Majesty's face is like a pear?" he asked. Thackeray thought that this argument convinced the judge; on the contrary, the artist was convicted.

The popular success of Philipon's magazine inspired the founding of *Punch,* subtitled *The London Charivari,* which appeared in 1841 with well-drawn political cartoons by John Leech, Richard Doyle, and (after Doyle resigned in protest against the editorial policy of attacking the Catholic Church), John Tenniel. A German counterpart, *Fliegender Blätter* (Falling Leaves) of Munich, made its debut three years later, much slicker in design but less political in content, and the Austrian *Kikeriki* (Rooster) came out in 1861.

Meantime America was proving to be barren soil for humor magazines, although it was hardly for lack of enterprise. In 1875, Brander Matthews was able to list forty-six such journals that had made an appearance.[5] They went by names like *The Brickbat, Cocktails,*

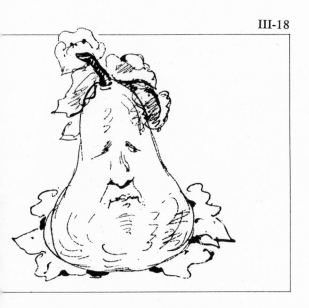

III-18

Diogenes hys Lanterne, Mrs. Grundy, Jubilee Days, Chic, The Kaleidoscope. Most never celebrated a first birthday; some never saw a second issue.

Following in the *Punch* tradition, most of these early American magazines used a standard cover design for all issues. (The covers for *The John-Donkey* and *The Lantern* were drawn by Felix O. C. Darley, a native of Philadelphia and the most accomplished native illustrator of his era.) But the publications' imitative quality was more than cover-deep. Some even adopted such titles as *American Punch, Southern Punch,* and *Punchinello.* The author of a bit of fiction published in 1870 has an undertaker say:

I've patched up all these graves, as well as them in the Ritual churchyard, and I know 'em all, sir. Over there, Editor of a Country Journal; next, Stockholder in Erie; next, Gentleman who undertook to be Guided in his Agriculture by Mr. [Horace] Greeley's 'What I know about farming'; next, Original Projector of American *Punch*; next, Proprietor of Rural Newspaper; next, another Projector of American *Punch*—indeed, all the rest of that row is American *Punches.* . . . [6]

Fittingly, the article was published in *Punchinello,* which was buried after nine months.

Although it was an error for the American magazines to choose European models, this was not the only reason for the high mortality rate. Even *Punchinello,* that rankest imitator, died less because New Yorkers were not

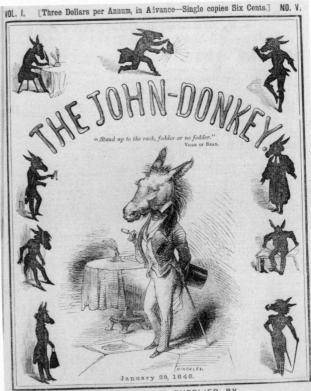

TOP III-19
Published July, 1846–October, 1847.

BOTTOM III-20
Published January 1– July 15, 1848.

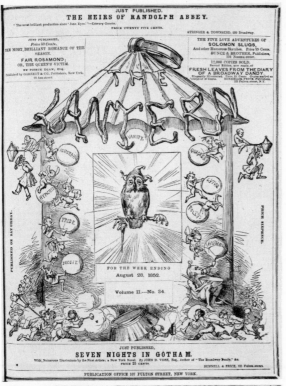

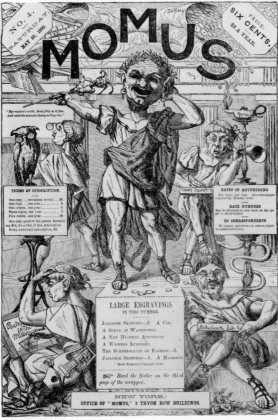

amused by a format designed to amuse Londoners than because the magazine was the mouthpiece of Tammany Hall and the Erie Railroad. (One *Punchinello* cartoon showed Boss Tweed smoking a pipe of peace and contentment on which sat a reporter. "Say, young man," asked the Tammany chief, "ain't you afraid you'll burn your breeches?") Jay Gould, Jim Fisk, Tweed, and his henchman Sweeny were said to have invested and lost $5000 each on the *Punchinello* venture.[7]

The failure of *Vanity Fair* (1859–63) was also in part the result of its policy of special pleading. Art editor Henry Louis Stephens, a transplanted Englishman, was a first-rate cartoonist, but his designs and the editorial policy of his brothers (the editor and the publisher) were too anti-Lincoln and anti-Negro for a nation engaged in a Civil War over slavery. On the other hand, some magazines might have failed because they were not controversial enough. One journal called *Uncle Sam* announced that "nothing immoral or scurrilous will ever appear in its columns. . . ." It lasted eleven issues![8]

The main cause of failure, however, was that most of the humor magazines just were not very humorous. As Richard Grant White wrote in 1862: "Many funerals are conducted in a manner far better calculated to minister to the sense of the ridiculous."[9]

TOP III-21   *Published January, 1852–July, 1853.*

BOTTOM III-22   *Published April–July, 1860.*

REMINISCENCES OF WASHINGTON,
DURING THE INAUGURATION. (BY OUR TRIANGLE.)

Our Triangle observes an excited Politician, who suddenly missing his antagonist in argument, encounters "the Beau" instead.

Outsiders wondering what the Inauguration Address is about

"Say, ol' fel', di-di-di ri leave my waw-waw-wallet here last night?"

Portrait executed by our Triangle early in the evening.

Another attempt a little later.

The last artistic effort of our Triangle.

III-23 *Known as the "Triangle" because of the way he signed his name, Frank Bellew (1828–1888) was sent to Washington by* The Lantern *to cover the inauguration of President Pierce and returned with these sketches.*

Yet there was one truly amusing cartoonist in this period. "Frank Bellew's pencil is extraordinary," commented Charles Dickens' London magazine, *All the Year Round*. "He probably originated more, of a purely comic nature, than all the rest of his artistic brethren put together."[10]

Incredibly prolific (despite his overly convivial habits), Bellew's art work appeared regularly in such publications as *The Lantern, Yankee Notions, Momus, The Reveille, Picayune, Vanity Fair*, the *Harper's* magazines, *Frank Leslie's Illustrated Newspaper, Phuniest of Phun* (which he edited), *Punchinello, Wild Oats, New York Daily Graphic, Scribner's, St. Nicholas*, and *Texas Siftings*. He was known as an "idea-monger" who also found time to write "innumerable sketches, stories, and short articles for the magazines and newspapers."[11]

Bellew, however, was hardly an "American" product. He had been born in India of an Irish father and an English mother, educated in France, worked as a London architect, and wrote a book about Scotland before arriving in the United States in 1850. His style was bright and even capable of pathos, but he never held strong convictions about the politics of his adopted country.

Another emigré who was to play a large part in our story arrived in New York two years before Bellew. Henry Carter, born in Ipswich, England, would pioneer illustrated journalism in America under the name "Frank Leslie." Trained as an engraver, Leslie speeded up the process of pictorial reporting by an ingenious, yet simple, device. When covering a fast-breaking event, he was able to get into print sooner than his competitors by dividing his pictures into sections and distributing parts among a number of engravers. In some illustrations thirty-two separate sections were pieced together.

He issued his first magazine in January, 1854—*Frank Leslie's Ladies' Gazette of Paris, London, and New York Fashions*. His most famous journal, *Frank Leslie's Illustrated Newspaper* (later called *Frank Leslie's Illustrated Weekly*), made its debut in late 1855. And after that there was a steady stream of *Frank Leslie's*, including such titles as *Champagne, The Cartoon, Jolly Joker, Chatterbox*, and *Pleasant Hours*.

Although the successful meshing of magazine publishing and political cartoons would not occur until the close of the Civil War, Frank Leslie and his stable of periodicals set the stage, both by first employing the artists who would usher in the golden age of American cartooning, notably Nast and Keppler, and by conditioning the country to a new style of lively journalism.

Toward the close of this period what the cartoonists lacked in talent was partly compensated for by their having a subject of infinite fascination. Abraham Lincoln's elongated, ungainly frame, his homely features, even his habit of spicing his speech with amusing stories were high-grade ore for the artists to mine.

What Lincoln thought of the cartonists is unknown. But he must have studied their work, for a cartoon that pictured him as Blondin crossing Niagara Falls on a high wire suggested a

III-24   *This pro-Lincoln cartoon saw McClellan as the joke, but the 1864 campaign also produced a biting "Copperhead" drawing that had Lincoln on a battlefield, surrounded by wounded soldiers, saying, "Now, Marshal, sing us 'Picayune Butler,' or something else that's funny."*

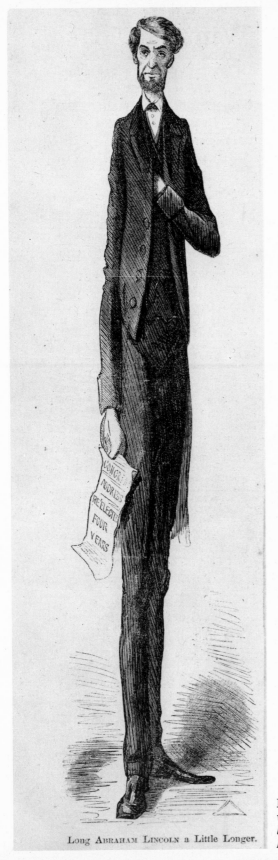

Long ABRAHAM LINCOLN a Little Longer.

metaphor that Lincoln was to use in an important meeting with a committee of senators.[12]

It has also been said that he was deeply hurt by a drawing of himself as Janus-faced in which his denial of Presidential ambitions in 1858 is contrasted with his quest for the nomination two years later (although the cartoon is so innocuous that it is difficult to believe it could sting a seasoned politician).[13]

Nor did the President have much cause to fear the pencil of southern artists. The few humor magazines put out in the Confederate states—*Southern Illustrated News* (Richmond), *Southern Punch* (Richmond), and *The Bugle Horn of Liberty* (Griffin, Georgia)—were pathetic documents. The most powerful cartooning from the southern standpoint was done by a German-born Baltimore dentist, Adalbert J. Volck, whose Civil War activities were shrouded in mystery—it being conflictingly reported that he fled to Europe (sending his work back by blockade-runner) and that the Federals threw him in jail at Fort McHenry.[14] In reality, in 1900 he wrote that his famous "Confederate War Etchings" were "done myself at night, after the days' unintermittent professional labor [in Baltimore.] Of course entire secrecy had to be preserved."[15] After the war Volck abandoned his artistic moonlighting to devote his full talents to dentistry

III-25   *Lincoln's reelection in 1864 was the event that made him "a little longer" in the opinion of cartoonist Frank Bellew.*

87

(his powerful physique allowing him to pull "out the big jaw tooth in a hurry," recalled a satisfied patient).[16]

Lincoln came under severest attack from the English cartoonists, who, reflecting the policy of their government, were unsympathetic to the North until late in the war. The American President's chief detractors were Sir John Tenniel (knighted in 1893) of *Punch* and Matt Morgan of *Fun*. Tenniel, who today is best known for his *Alice in Wonderland* illustrations, was *Punch*'s

III-26 *Dr. Volck shows Lincoln, the clown, presenting a Comedy of Death.*

III-27 *Lincoln's difficulty in finding a general provided the inspiration for one of the rare hits in the* Southern Illustrated News, *1863.*

MASTER ABRAHAM LINCOLN GETS A NEW TOY.

chief cartoonist for forty years. The magazine's cartoons were always collectively arrived at during the famous Wednesday night editorial dinners, but Tenniel executed his colleagues' ideas with a chaste severity. As a proper Victorian gentleman with a Blimpish moustache, Sir John developed the lion as a symbol of the British Empire and left an estate of a half-million dollars.

Matt Morgan, an actor's son, was a very different sort. In 1867 he became part owner of *Tomahawk*, whose fame derived mainly from his incendiary cartoons, one of which made daring reference to the Prince of Wales' debauchery. Later, when Morgan moved to New York, his studio would be fondly remembered by fellow artists for its claret-filled washtub. Although Tenniel drew Lincoln with the outline of a devil's horns, Morgan's renderings were the more vicious.

Yet when Lincoln was assassinated

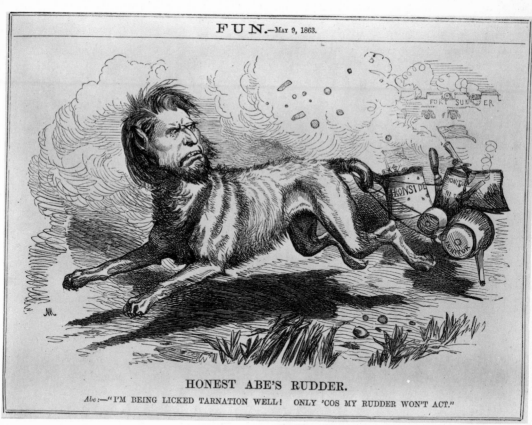

FUN.—May 9, 1863.

HONEST ABE'S RUDDER.

Abe:—"I'M BEING LICKED TARNATION WELL! ONLY 'COS MY RUDDER WON'T ACT."

III-28 *Morgan's cartoon came after the Union failed to capture Charleston, 1863.*

the English cartoonists paid him most eloquent tribute. The obituary cartoon was a Tenniel composition, and his best-known showed Britannia laying a wreath on Lincoln's bier. Under the drawing was an eleven-stanza poem by Tom Taylor, *Punch*'s editor, in which the magazine reproaches itself for its attitude toward Lincoln. This effort, however, was not without opposition. Shirley Brooks, a future *Punch* editor, wrote in his diary, "Dined Punch. All there. Let out my views against some verses on Lincoln in which T. T. had not only made P. eat humble pie, but swallow dish and all."

ABE LINCOLN'S LAST CARD; OR, ROUGE-ET-NOIR.

III-29 *Tenniel saw the Emancipation Proclamation as nothing more than a gesture by a wily gambler, 1862.*

III-30 *Sir John Tenniel's "Britannia
Sympathises with Columbia," and three
stanzas from Tom Taylor's poem.*
Punch, *May 6, 1865.*

You *lay a wreath on murdered Lincoln's bier,*
    You, who with mocking pencil wont to trace,
Broad for the self-complacent British sneer,
    His length of shambling limb, his furrowed face.

Beside this corpse, that bears for winding sheet
    The stars and stripes he lived to rear anew,
Between the mourners at his head and feet,
    Say, scurril jester, is there room for you?

Yes, he had lived to shame me from my sneer,
    To lame my pencil, and confute my pen—
To make me own this hind of princes peer,
    This rail-splitter a true born king of men.

IV-1

IV

Magazines
1866-96

America's premier political cartoonist was born in 1840 in the barracks town of Landau, where his father was a trombone player in the Bavarian army. He was six when he arrived in New York; he was sixteen when he became a staff artist on *Frank Leslie's Illustrated Newspaper;* he was twenty-four when, during the Civil War, President Lincoln said of him, "Thomas Nast has been our best recruiting sergeant."

In 1862 Nast joined *Harper's Weekly,* and for the next quarter-century his name would be inextricably joined with that self-styled "Journal of Civilization." Harper & Brothers started a monthly magazine in 1850 designed to avoid political controversy, serialize English novels, and promote the firm's books. Seven years later, after Frank Leslie had demonstrated that there was a large market for an illustrated weekly, the Harper boys entered the field and, under the editorship of George William Curtis, turned *Harper's Weekly* into "the fighting arm" of their publishing house.

The magazine became the greatest political power in post-bellum publishing because of Nast and Curtis; yet the fiery German refugee and the Puritan son of a New York banker formed an uneasy collaboration. Nast once said

IV-2

that when Curtis "attacks a man with his pen it seems as if he were apologizing for the act." By contrast, the cartoonist continued, "I try to hit the enemy between the eyes and knock him down." On the editor's part, he always felt there was something ungentleman-

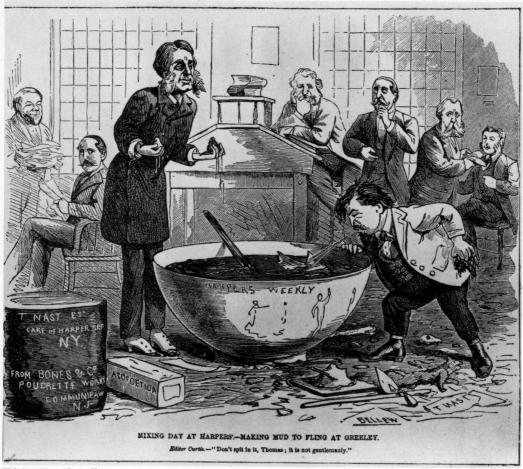

MIXING DAY AT HARPERS'.—MAKING MUD TO FLING AT GREELEY.

Editor Curtis.—"Don't spit in it, Thomas; it is not gentlemanly."

IV-3 *Frank Bellew captures the interplay between Nast and Curtis (as the Harper Brothers look on). Nast apparently did not hold this drawing against Bellew, for he later sent his fellow cartoonist a check when he heard he was sick and in financial straits.*

ly about a political cartoon. It was so stark, so final, so incapable of suggesting "but on the other hand . . . ."

Hired as a battlefield illustrator, Nast gradually sought compositions that went beyond events to the deeper meaning of the Civil War. One of these "emblematic" messages, which appeared shortly after the Democratic National Convention in 1864 adopted a peace platform, was entitled "Compromise with the South." As J. V. Whitaker wrote in 1876, "Seldom has an artist achieved fame as suddenly as Nast did by this single effort."[1] Nast's eloquent indictment of the northern appeasers

IV-4

was reproduced by the millions as a Republican campaign document, and, in the opinion of Rufus Rockwell Wilson, "did as much as any other event to assure the reelection of Mr. Lincoln."[2]

But Nast's fame was to rest mainly on some fifty drawings he did in 1871 when, in tandem with the equally Jovian wrath of *The New York Times*, he brought down the mighty "Boss" Tweed and his Tammany Ring. Nast's bold designs and elaborate crosshatching, which might overwhelm a humble subject, were ideally suited for crimes of Tammany proportions. (The Ring

charged New York City $2,870,464.06 for the nine-month labors of one plasterer! Commented the *Times*: "He could afford to donate the .06 to charity.")

IV-5   In this single figure—unusual for a Nast design—the artist has created the perfect cartoon: the idea is humorous; the drawing is well executed; the message is valid; the symbolism is clear, but not (yet) a cliché. Besides Tweed's obesity, by this stage in Nast's campaign he is able to identify the Boss merely by his $15,500 diamond stickpin with the hint of features in the $.

THE "BRAINS"

95

IV-6 *Unsurpassed for raw
power—it measured
14" x 20"—this was the
climax of the campaign,
appearing in the last* Harper's
before the election. The Times
*called it "the most impressive
political picture ever
produced in this country." It
is also the first appearance of
the Tammany Tiger, which
Nast adopted from the
insignia of Tweed's volunteer
fire company. (Nast was paid
$150 for such double-page
cartoons.)*

IV-7 *It was a frequent Nast technique to caption his cartoons with statements by the men he was attacking. "It will soon blow over" was a remark of Mayor O. K. Hall (the vulture with eyeglasses).*

HARPER'S WEEKLY.
A JOURNAL OF CIVILIZATION

Vol. XV.—No. 775.] NEW YORK, SATURDAY, OCTOBER 21, 1871. [WITH A SUPPLEMENT. PRICE TEN CENTS.

THE ONLY THING THEY RESPECT OR FEAR.

IV-9 *Nast's triumphant comment on the election results shows Mayor Hall still clinging to the remains of the building since no vote had been taken on his office. Hall was considered the least culpable of the Tweed Ring and ended his days writing for the comic magazines.*

IV-8 *This ran in the same issue as "The Brains." Nast drew as many as six anti-Tweed cartoons for a single* Harper's Weekly. *In retaliation, the Ring rejected all Harper books for use in the school system, a serious financial blow to the firm.*

THE AMERICAN RIVER GANGES.

IV-10   *Nast meant this as an indictment of sectarianism in the public schools and of Tammany's "sacrifice" of children's education for Catholic votes. Nast's attitude toward the Roman Church was shared by the other great nineteenth-century American cartoonist, Joseph Keppler, a birthright Catholic.*

Although Nast acquired the reputation of a reformer from the Tammany series, his career was checkered and difficult to categorize. In 1884, when he deserted his party to support Cleveland over Blaine, he was again allied with the so-called Good Government element. But he was in the forefront of the Radical Republican effort to impeach President Johnson (see II–28 for Nast on "King Andy"), he refused to budge in his loyalty to the Grant Administration even when the full story of its corruption and incompetence was known, and his deep suspicion of the Catholic Church bordered on bigotry.

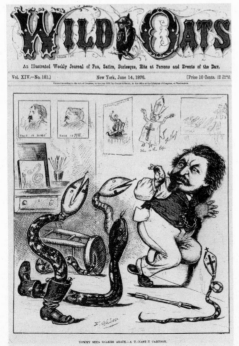

IV-11   *Nineteen-year-old Frederick Opper's satire on Nast's Catholic phobia also suggests that Nast's style was an imitation of the French illustrator Gustave Doré. (*Wild Oats *paid $20 for a cover cartoon.)*

Nast's cartoons were a major circulation builder for *Harper's Weekly*. (The fight with Tweed tripled the magazine's readership.) Rival Frank Leslie's response was to bring Matt Morgan from London, where his caricatures of Lincoln had earned a reputation for invective (see III–34). The first Presidential campaign in which Nast and Morgan squared off against each other was the Grant–Greeley canvass of 1872. Billed as a sort of heavyweight championship of cartoonists, it turned out to be "no contest." The transplanted Englishman had little understanding of American politics; indeed, one observer claimed that he "never learned how to draw an American face: all his figures, good or bad, were cockneys of the purest water."[3] Morgan's work degenerated into leaden-handed attacks on Grant's drinking habits (see II–24). Later Morgan abandoned cartooning altogether to become a decorator of pottery and a designer of very good theatrical lithographs.

The Nast caricatures of Greeley, on the other hand, were less personal, more humorous, but equally savage. Horace Greeley, the brilliant if eccentric editor who was the Democratic and Liberal Republican candidate, was fair game, of course; yet when he died shortly after the election there were many who believed that Nast's thundering pencil had been the instrument of death.[4]

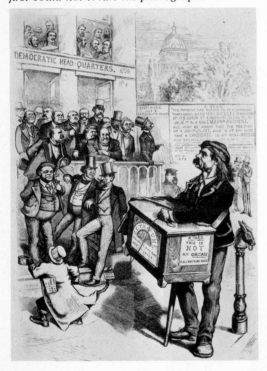

IV-12 *Nast's campaign against Greeley begin mildly enough with the Democratic candidate pictured as dancing to the tune of Whitelaw Reid, who had succeeded him as editor of the New York* Tribune. *Gratz Brown, the Vice Presidential candidate, is represented as a tag (see monkey's tail) because Nast at first could not locate his photograph.*

"LET US CLASP HANDS OVER THE BLOODY CHASM."—HORACE GREELEY.

IV-13   *Greeley—the man in the white duster—was a liberal in his attitude toward the recently defeated South, which inspired Nast to "wave the bloody shirt."*

IV-14   *Nast's last cartoon of the campaign was considered particularly heartless because Greeley's wife had just died and he was very ill. He died three weeks later.*

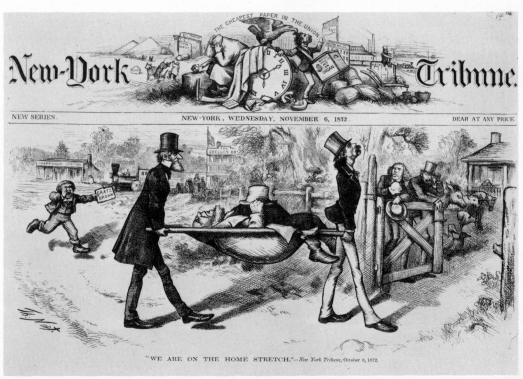

"WE ARE ON THE HOME STRETCH."—*New York Tribune*, October 9, 1872.

While Nast's handling of the Greeley campaign was particularly distressing to the gentle Curtis, publisher Fletcher Harper was able, as he had been before, to smooth over their differences. But after Harper's death in 1877 the cartoonist and the editor had more and more difficulty reconciling their approaches to issues and personalities. Finally, in 1887, Nast left the magazine. "In quitting *Harper's Weekly*," said Henry Watterson, "Nast lost his forum; in losing him, *Harper's Weekly* lost its political influence." There was more than a little truth in the remark. The magazine would never again be so powerful, although the cartoonist's departure was not the sole reason for its decline; and Nast, whose investments and business enterprises turned sour, was ultimately forced to accept the modest position of U.S. consul to Guayaquil, Equador (in order "to learn how to pronounce its name," he said).

Part of Nast's personal tragedy—in that he was famous in his youth and forgotten in his last years—was the direct result of his strength as an artist. For his raw, impassioned approach to politics could not be taken by the public in prolonged doses.

Nast was a rare, isolated phenomenon. He left no disciples or school of cartooning, as Keppler would do; yet, in a sense, every cartoonist was his disciple, freely adopting the symbols he invented and, more importantly, having greater acceptance merely because there had been a Thomas Nast.

At about the time that Nast's popularity began to wane in the mid-1880s, a new cartoonist had captured the fancy of the American public. His work was less cumbersome than Nast's, gayer and more graceful; hardly likely to incite riot, still capable of drawing blood. Joseph Keppler's weapon was the rapier, not the broadsword.

The son of a Viennese baker (his earliest artistry was the ornamentation on his father's cakes), Keppler's principle occupation was that of actor when he arrived in St. Louis in 1867 at the age of twenty-nine. But after a fling on the American stage and the founding of two short-lived humor magazines, in 1872 he joined Frank Leslie's stable of artists in New York. Then, in 1876, Keppler again tried his hand at publishing, this time with a German language weekly called *Puck,* to which he added an English edition the next year.

IV-15 *In May, 1902, Nast pictured himself as leaving for Ecuador, where he was greeted by "Yellow Jack Will D. H. [deadhead] you." In December, as he predicted, Nast died of yellow fever.*

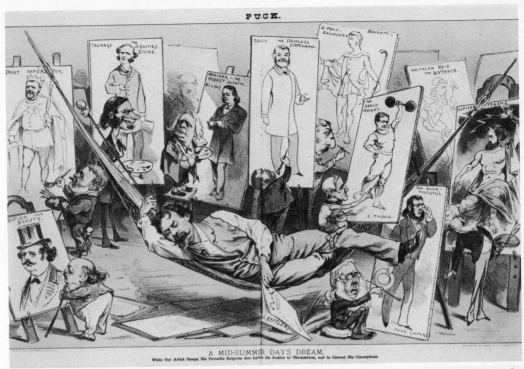

A MID-SUMMER DAY'S DREAM.

While Our Artist Sleeps, His Favorite Subjects Are Left to Do Justice to Themselves, and to Correct His Conceptions.

IV-16 *Joseph Keppler of the curly hair and well-waxed mustache paints himself for* Puck, *1881.*

IV-17 *The first English edition introduces Puck, a masthead figure that the artist modeled after his daughter. (See detail below.) Besides doing all the cartoons, Keppler drew intricate advertisements for such clients as a wholesale upholsterer and an importer of Hungarian wines.*

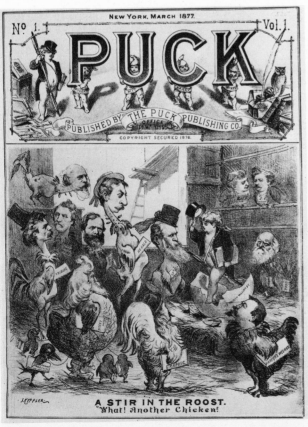

Puck was different right from the start. It was bigger: twice the size of the humor magazines that Americans had known, nearly the dimensions of the current *Life*. Parts of it were in color, whereas its predecessors had been all black and white. Its covers, instead of the traditional design, stepped forward each week sporting a different cartoon. There was also something a bit exotic about the newcomer, perhaps an air of Viennese gaity that Keppler and his imported artists—F. Graetz and Karl Edler von Stur—brought to their creations. (Graetz, it was said, spoke no English and cartoon ideas had to be translated into German for his benefit.)[5] By the early eighties *Puck's* circulation had risen to 80,000, and in 1883 Keppler's financial interest in the magazine was placed at $600,000.[6]

Keppler the tycoon, however, was also a steady-handed editor who gathered an art staff of remarkably high competence, including, at various times, such luminaries as Frederick Opper, James A. Wales, Bernard Gillam, Eugene Zimmerman, Louis Dalrymple, C. J. Taylor, Frank A. Nankivell, Louis M. Glackens, J. S. Pughe, and Joseph Keppler, Jr.

It is hard to overestimate the political influence of *Puck* and its rival, *Judge*, during the last two decades of the nineteenth century. Joseph B. Bishop thought it greater than all the daily newspapers combined. "Their

---

THE 13-15-14 PUZZLE IN THE SENATE.
SENATORS MERRY OVER A CARTOON PUZZLE WHICH SENATOR CONKLING COULD NOT SOLVE.

[BY TELEGRAPH TO THE TRIBUNE.]

WASHINGTON, March 17.—During the morning hour to-day somebody sent Senator Blaine a copy of *Puck* containing a cartoon representing Senator Conkling, with an elongated and very lugubrious expression, playing the 15 puzzle with blocks bearing the faces of probable and improbable Presidential candidates.

A broad smile rippled over the Senator's face as he took in the fun of the thing, and other Senators near him glanced over the paper and shared in the merriment. Soon a group of four or five had gathered about Senator Blaine's desk, and others who sauntered that way glanced at the cartoon, and walked off laughing to the cloak room.

Shortly afterward the paper began its travels. When it reached Senator David Davis, Senator Conkling walked up, and the Senator from Illinois gravely pointed out the figures and explained the situation as he understood it. Senator Conkling, who had evidently never solved the 15 puzzle, did not seem to understand it, and soon walked away and resumed his seat.

Those who have wrestled with the puzzle will appreciate the fun of the thing when it is explained that in the cartoon Grant represents 15, Blaine 14, and Tilden 13, and they are so arranged on the board that, move whichever way the player may, one of the two latter seems bound to come in at the end.

IV-18

---

weekly cartoons were awaited eagerly, were passed from hand to hand, and were the subject of animated comment in all political circles."[7]

Puck's first engagement in Presidential politics began in a near-disastrous fashion for a magazine that customarily had a ten-day gap between conception and publication of the massive color lithographs that were its trademark and that graced its front and back

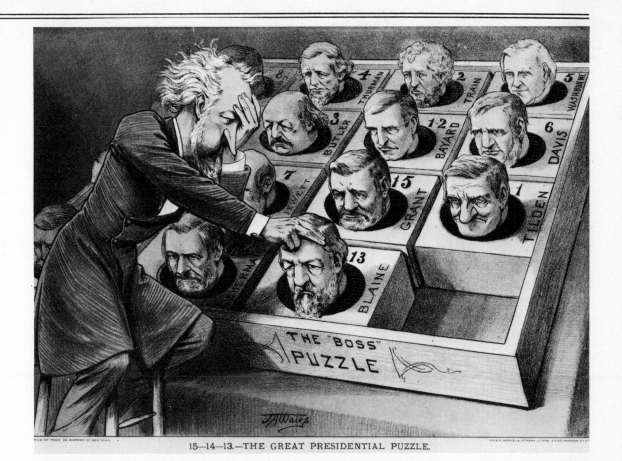

15—14—13.—THE GREAT PRESIDENTIAL PUZZLE.

covers and its centerfold. In 1880, as the Republicans convened in Chicago, *Puck* artists began drawing "to meet every possible contingency." As an editorial stated, "We were ready for any nomination that the Convention could make—Grant, Blaine, Sherman, Washburne, Edmunds—it didn't matter; we had cartoons laid out for every one— even for the off-chance men—Private Dalzell and Hamilton Fish."[8] On the thirty-sixth ballot the G.O.P. finally made up its mind, and, unfortunately for *Puck*, it settled on a candidate whom the magazine had not considered a "possible contingency"—James A. Garfield. (The lesson learned from this experience was to run a puzzle cartoon when an election or nomination was in doubt.)

But there was nothing enigmatic about "Forbidding the Banns," the most notorious cartoon of the campaign. Americans were not shocked by the suggestion of a Presidential candidate being involved in a financial scandal—that was an often-aired charge—but putting Garfield in the garb of an unwed mother was considered Rabelaisian for the times.

The next Presidential campaign has been correctly called "the highwater line of the element of purely personal abuse in [American] comic art."[9] Its tone was set by what a senator from Kansas called "the most merciless and fatal" cartoon representation of a public man—James G. Blaine as the Tattooed Man.[10] The first appearance of the Republican candidate displaying on his body the charges that had been made against him was in the April 16, 1884, issue of *Puck*. Drawn by Bernard Gillam and thought up at an editorial meeting, the cartoon proved an instant sensation. Literary critic Harry Thruston Peck, speaking for many who lived through that election, recalled in 1900 how it made him "feel a certain irresistible thrill of loathing."[11] Repeated time after time, the Tattooed Man became famous enough to give rise to many conflicting claims over its paternity. Various writers stated that the idea had come from the magazine's business manager, the editor of *Puck*'s German edition, even the office boy! "It indicated what an office boy can do if he has opportunity."[12] Perhaps the

IV-20 *From left to right: W. H. Barnum, chairman, Democratic National Committee; Murat Halstead, editor,* Cincinnati Commercial; *Carl Schurz, Secretary of the Interior; Whitelaw Reid, editor, New York* Tribune; *James A. Garfield; Senator Don Cameron, Pennsylvania; George Robeson, New Jersey congressman; Senator John A. Logan, Illinois; Senator Roscoe Conkling, New York.*

IV-21 Puck *turned Garfield's opponent, General Winfield S. Hancock, into a political Samson, although Keppler claimed he would have preferred that the Democrats had nominated the shopworn Samuel Tilden because he was so easy to caricature. The campaign was more agonizing for Republican cartoonist Nast since Hancock was a personal friend. Nast treated him gently.*

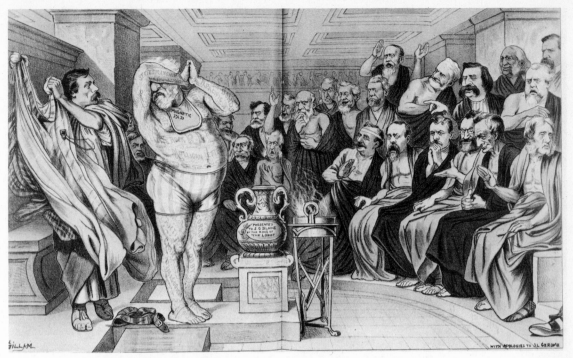

IV-22 *Blaine wanted to sue* Puck *for libel, and only the strongest pressure from his friends dissuaded him from going to court.*

    The cartoon is a takeoff on a painting by Gérôme that had been a Paris sensation a dozen years earlier and is based on the story of the Greek orator Hypereides, who won a verdict for the courtesan Phryne by exposing her beauty to the court.

IV-23, IV-24 *Despite the tales of supposed "eye witnesses," the genesis of Gillam's Tattooed Man of 1884 was clearly Keppler's earlier attacks on Grant —in 1875 (below) and in 1876 (right).*

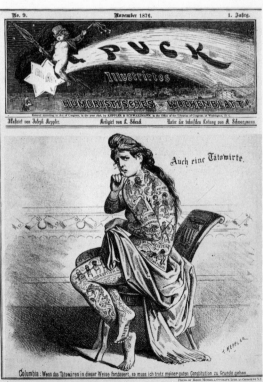

Another voice for Cleveland.

IV-25   *The Republicans tried to counter the Tattooed Man campaign by circulating a story that Grover Cleveland had fathered an illegitimate child. Later, cartoonist Frank Beard, as if to repent for his part in the 1884 canvass, became the artist for a Chicago religious magazine called* Ram's Horn *and "used the pen of caricature as a champion of Christian living."*

grandest irony of the cartoon's history was that its artist, Gillam, was a staunch Republican and actually voted for Blaine.

It was Keppler's design to introduce a recurring symbol or theme into each Presidential contest—Hancock as Samson in 1880, Blaine as the Tattooed Man in 1884. And in 1888, when Benjamin Harrison, a man of modest stature and the grandson of "Old Tippecanoe," was the Republican nominee, the *Puck* cartoonist invented his most amusing device—Grandpa's Hat.

In 1881 James A. Wales, a *Puck* artist (of the 15—puzzle fame) with a special gift for portraiture, had a quar-

rel with Keppler and left to found a rival magazine, *Judge*. Wales was never able to put his journal on a firm financial footing, and in late 1885 he sold out to a promoter named William J. Arkell, who promptly lured Bernard Gillam away from *Puck* by making him a full partner. (*Puck* now had a vacant cartoonist's chair; Wales now was out of a job. So Keppler and Wales resolved their differences, and Wales returned to *Puck*, where he remained until his early death in 1886.)

Gillam, *Judge*'s new chief cartoonist, had been born in England and brought to the United States at an early age. His partner Arkell, who was also to become

IV-26, IV-27   *Over the years Keppler kept enlarging Grandpa's Hat so that by 1890 (in "The Raven," below left) it overwhelmed the second Harrison President, and by 1892, as the logical conclusion to the series, "Little Ben" had disappeared altogether, and Uncle Sam asks, "Where is he?"*

his brother-in-law, would write long after Gillam's death: "He was a poor boy, and for much of his youthful period he did not even have a place in which to sleep. Many a night he spent in one or another of the parks of New York, and it follows that often he went hungry also. One day, when he was seated on a park bench drawing a picture, Henry Ward Beecher happened along. The great preacher no doubt noted Gillam's poverty, as it must have been disclosed in his attire, and the boy's artistic impulse attracted him. Entering into conversation with Gillam, Beecher learned his circumstances and at once took more than a casual interest in him. Through Beecher's influence Gillam was sent to an art school, where he developed as a cartoonist very rapidly." [13]

Judge's primary contribution to the lore of American politics was the popularization in 1900 of the Full Dinner Pail, a symbol invented by Grant Hamilton, "a big-bodied, big-hearted man, beloved of all the [*Judge*] artists," according to James Montgomery Flagg. "He was, moreover, the kind of a man whose face proclaims that he could not do an ignoble act." [14] Hamilton, the magazine's leading cartoonist after the death of Bernard Gillam in 1896, was ably assisted by Eugene Zimmerman ("Zim"), a designer of hysterical grotesqueries, who had been a sign painter when discovered by Keppler and whom

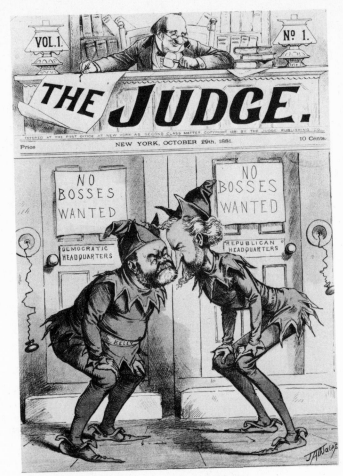

IV-28 *James Wales tried to cast* Judge *in a politically impartial role, as the cover of his first issue shows, but when Arkell and Gillam took over they made it into a Republican journal designed to counter the influence of the Democratic* Puck.

BENJAMIN "WHERE AM I AT?"

IV-29   *Convinced that Harrison would win reelection in 1892, Gillam prepared a double-page cartoon of Cleveland's being run over by the G.O.P. elephant, which was on the press when the news of the Democrats' smashing victory reached the* Judge *office. Gillam quickly doctored the cut, changing Cleveland's face to Harrison's, adding an "overwhelming defeat" eyepatch to the elephant, and generally trying to make his drawing reflect the altered situation. The artist also drew himself as a monkey turning a somersault (lower left).*

IV-30, IV-31   *The Full Dinner Pail, that symbol of humble prosperity to which William McKinley claimed he owed his reelection, as drawn by* Judge *artists Grant Hamilton (left) and Victor Gillam.*

Gillam brought with him from *Puck*, and by Gillam's younger brother, who had signed his work "F. Victor" or "Victor" until Bernard's death, after which he reclaimed the family name.

Two years after the founding of *Judge*, the last of the great triumvirate of late-nineteenth-century humor magazines made its appearance. *Puck* and *Judge* had been primarily political, attempting only halfheartedly to comment on the customs and manners of the American society. It was left to *Life* to fill this void. And the new magazine did so not only with the bubbling enthusiasm of the very young but also with a sophistication that belied its founders' years.

Life was the product of *Harvard Lampoon* graduates—its early issues not surprisingly bear a striking resemblance to that college humor magazine—and its guiding spirit was John Ames Mitchell, known to his artists as "The General." While the magazine's tone was social, politics were not entirely overlooked, and its pages featured cartoons on the political scene by Francis G. Attwood, William H. Walker, Oliver Herford, Palmer Cox, E. W. Kemble, W. H. Hyde, Otho Cushing, Charles Kendrick, F. T. Richards, William A. Rogers, and Charles Dana Gibson.

In the nineteenth century (as today), the materials from which the cartoonists mined their political similes and analogies were determined by their own interests and education and those of their audiences. A man crossed Niagara Falls on a tightrope, baseball be-

IV-32 *John Mitchell's own cartoons had an airy quality that would be* Life's *trademark, and at first the editor did most of his magazine's artwork.*

IV-33 *Although William H. Walker gives two views of* Life's *John A. Mitchell, the editor was considered a master at the art of the graceful rejection.*

Rejected   J. A. M.   Accepted

AN HEIR TO THE THRONE,
OR THE NEXT REPUBLICAN CANDIDATE

IV-34   *When showman Barnum reopened his New York Museum in 1860 it featured a deformed Negro boy whom he named "What Is It?" and advertised as "the connecting link between man and the ape."*

One man who was always sure to provide cartoonists with material in the mid-nineteenth century was P. T. Barnum.

IV-35   *Midgets Tom Thumb and Commodore Nutt were international celebrities as well as rivals for the hand of little Lavinia Warren, another member of Barnum's troupe.*

came a fever, the Prince of Prussia made a grand tour of the American continent, a book about Uncle Tom became a best seller—these were the current happenings that people talked about, and, hence, the events on which political cartoons were grafted.

The cartoonists—especially Nast, Keppler, and Gillam—were extremely fond of the literary allusion. They turned for inspiration to the Bible and *The Arabian Nights,* Cervantes and Aesop. But their favorite was Shakespeare. Any random sampling of nine-teenth-century cartoons is sure to turn up Lincoln as Othello, Polk as Macbeth, or Tweed as Falstaff.

Nor, of course, did cartoonists any longer have to direct their fire primarily at the major political figures. The changeover from engraving to lithography had allowed them the luxury of caricaturing the fleeting event or personage without bankrupting their publications. Some public men got undue attention for the obvious reason that they had physically outstanding characteristics. One such gentleman caused

IV-36   *General George McClellan as Hamlet, 1864.*

"I KNEW HIM, HORATIO; A FELLOW OF INFINITE JEST. * * * WHERE BE YOUR GIBES NOW?—*Hamlet, Act IV., Scene 1.*

THE PATH OF DUTY.
STAR-ROUTERS:—"Be rul'd, you shall not go!"
HAMLET-ARTHUR:—I say, away! Go on, I'll follow thee!"

THE LATEST VERSION.
HAMLET CROKER (to GHOST TWEED).—I'll follow thee!

IV-37 *President Chester Arthur as Hamlet, 1881.*

IV-38 *Democratic boss Richard Croker as Hamlet, 1894.*

IV-39 *Republican boss Mark Hanna as Hamlet, 1899.*

IV-40 *President Theodore Roosevelt as Hamlet, 1907.*

HANNALET, PRINCE OF $MARK IN THE MODERN GRAVEYARD SCENE.

TEDLET'S SOLILOQUY.

cartoonist Oliver Herford to burst into verse:

I'm sorry William Taft is out
Of Politics; without a doubt
Of all the Presidential crew
He was the easiest to do.[15]

Why, after years of publishing failures, did *Puck, Judge,* and *Life* suddenly emerge within a six-year span? John Ames Mitchell, whose opinion should be highly valued, felt that the magazines' successes were the direct result of the "aesthetic wave" that swept over the United States after the Civil War, affecting, as he said, everything "from a railway-car to a shirt-button." "It was a grand movement," the founder of *Life* concluded. "It not only taught us

A HARMLESS EXPLOSION.

IV-41 *Joseph Keppler's favorite second-echelon politician was Roscoe Conkling, whose resignation from the Senate in 1881 inspired "A Harmless Explosion." Keppler also portrayed the tall, arrogant New Yorker as a peacock and a stork. To Matt Morgan he was a pouter pigeon, while on the cover of* Harper's Weekly *he was, at various times, goat, lamb, and jackdaw.*

IV-42 *Life's Francis G. Attwood made a specialty of caricaturing cockeyed Benjamin Butler. While the politician-soldier was notoriously impervious to criticism, he was supposed to have been deeply hurt by a cartoon that turned his eyes into silver spoons—a reference to the charge that he had "stolen spoons" while occupying New Orleans during the Civil War.*

IV-43　The Verdict, *a
Democratic magazine
(1898–1900), shows the
House Speaker, Republican
Thomas Reed, in a less than
flattering light, although
cartoonist Mirs resisted the
common practice of perching
a crown on the bald head of
the so-called "Czar" (see
II-26).*

"CZAR" REED IS READY.

to think for ourselves, but the standard of taste has ever since been perceptibly higher."[16] Fairfax Downey felt that Mitchell succeeded because he "had chosen the psychological period when a nation which had taken itself soberly and seriously for a hundred years was proudly discovering and vaunting its sense of humor."[17] Others thought that the magazines came when the general business climate was good and that publishing, like many other industries, merely benefited from an expanding economy.[18] Possibly the magazines did appear at the right moment aesthetically, psychologically, and economically. But there was another, more important, reason for their successes: quality. As James L. Ford said of *Puck*—and it applied also to *Judge* and *Life*: "It shot folly as it flew, punctured shams, and dealt with politics and other matters of serious import fearlessly, sincerely, and, on the whole, truthfully."[19]

Later, as Alexander King would write of these magazines, "They became arrogant, conservative, and stuffy, and losing complete sight of their prime functions as humorous weeklies, they standardized their material until it lost all contact with the turbulent life and reality about them." But this was not until the World War I period. The first sign of decline had nothing to do with their own failings. Rather it was because of the rise of a powerful competitor—the daily newspaper.

V-1   *"Death of the Embargo," New York* Evening Post, *1814. A terrapin represents the Embargo; the man who has severed its head is President James Madison.*

V
Newspapers
1884-1968

Three years before Keppler founded *Puck* in 1876, Frederick Hudson stated in his *History of Journalism* that the American public did not support comic weeklies because "no one can wait a week to laugh; it must come in daily with our coffee." Yet until the 1880s one form of humor—the cartoon—was notable for its absence in the daily newspaper. True, there had been occasional newspaper cartoons ever since Franklin's "Join or Die." The first cartoon series appeared in the *Massachusetts Centinel* during the fight for ratification of the U.S. Constitution, and at odd intervals other papers resorted to political caricature, such as the 1814 pictorial comment on the Embargo Act which appeared in the New York *Evening Post*.

Still cartoons were expensive and painfully slow to produce; newspaper type, moreover, was set in narrow columns and the presses made it inconvenient to print anything larger than one column in width—a space too con-fining for an effective cartoon.

Then in 1867 James Gordon Bennett, Jr., founded the New York *Evening Telegram*. Printed on pink paper and featuring gory murders and sexual escapades, Bennett's product, wrote his biographer, "obviously was designed to appeal to readers who tended to move their lips when they read it."[1] The *Telegram* also ran a big front-page cartoon every Friday, making the newspaper the first daily in the country to use cartoons on a regular basis.

The great breakthrough for the newspaper cartoon came five days before the Presidential election of 1884 when Joseph Pulitzer's New York *World* printed "The Royal Feast of Belshazzar," an interpretation of a plutocratic dinner that had been held the night before at Delmonico's in honor of the Republican candidate, James G. Blaine. The drawing by Walt McDougall, although crude and artless, created a sensation. The Democrats reproduced it on thousands of billboards in the Empire State. Since

V-2   *From the "Federal Edifice" Series,* Massachusetts Centinel, *1788.*

THE DAILY GRAPHIC

AN ILLUSTRATED EVENING NEWSPAPER

39 & 41 PARK PLACE

VOL. IV. | All the News. Four Editions Daily. | NEW YORK, SATURDAY, APRIL 25, 1874.---TRIPLE SHEET. | $12 Per Year in Advance. Single Copies, Five Cents. | NO. 355.

THE MODERN LAOCOON.

V-3 *New York's* Daily Graphic, *published from March 4, 1873, until
January 4, 1888, was the first fully illustrated newspaper in the United States.
Although this cartoon is by old pro Frank Bellew, the* Graphic *provided
an opportunity for many younger artists, including Livingston Hopkins,
A. B. Frost, C. J. Taylor, W. A. Rogers, M. A. Woolf, E. W. Kemble, and
Walt McDougall.*

Blaine would have been elected if he had carried New York and since he lost New York by a mere 1100 votes, it was not uncommon to hear that this cartoon was responsible for elevating Grover Cleveland to the White House.

Hungarian-born Joseph Pulitzer, publisher of the St. Louis *Post-Dispatch,* had entered the New York newspaper market in 1883 by buying the listless *World* from Jay Gould. Deter-

mined to turn his new paper into a national force by making it the spokesman for the working man, he dressed the *World* in lively eye-catching graphics—news illustrations, cartoons, and comics. Pulitzer's success inspired young William Randolph Hearst, son of a California senator and mine owner, who came east in 1895 to pump his father's millions into the moribund New York *Journal.* In the Great Circu-

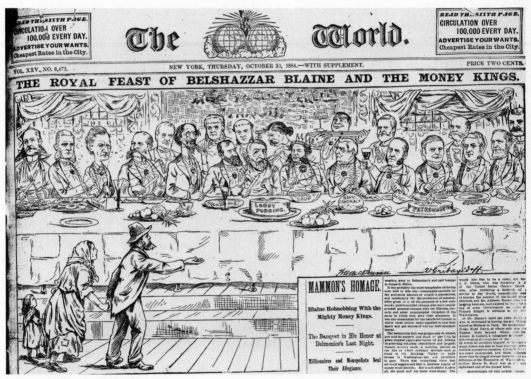

V-4 *Many of the faces in McDougall's famous cartoon were done by Valerian Gribayedoff, a Russian-born soldier of fortune who had fought in a Chilean revolution. A specialist in portraiture, Gribayedoff once engaged an assistant to do nothing but draw whiskers and eyebrows!*

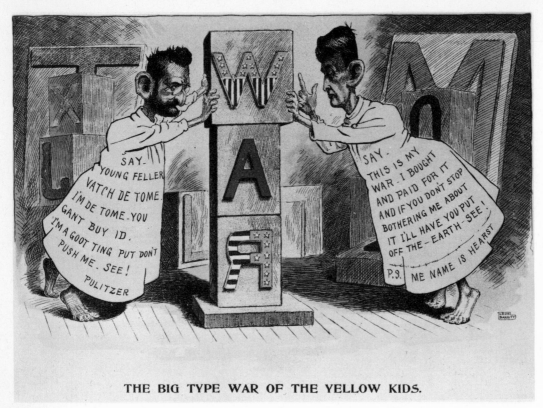

THE BIG TYPE WAR OF THE YELLOW KIDS.

V-5

lation War that followed, Hearst had the resources to hire away some of Pulitzer's best talent, including Richard Outcault, creator of *The Yellow Kid.* (See I-14.)

The insurrection in Cuba that had been simmering for several years, provided Hearst and Pulitzer with the excuse for a rip-roaring circulating-building crusade. Playing on the American people's sympathy for the *insurrectos*, Hearst artists drew fake atrocity pictures of Spaniards stripping American women on the high seas, while Pulitzer correspondents in Cuba cabled reports of "Blood on the roadsides, blood in the fields, blood on the doorsteps, blood, blood, blood."

In 1899 Hearst lured to the *Journal* one of the funniest political cartoonists in the annals of the art in America. For sheer good humor and clownishness, for sugar-coating barbs and disguising a sting with an aura of innocent droll-

THE SPANISH BRUTE
ADDS MUTILATION TO MURDER.

OUR EXPANSIVE UNCLE.
BUT IT'S ONLY TEMPORARY.

V-6 *Most cartoonists followed the Hearst–Pulitzer lead in promoting war with Spain. The viciousness that Grant Hamilton displayed week after week in* Judge *was not atypical. After the sinking of the* Maine, *sales of Hearst's* Journal *shot up to over one million copies a day and Pulitzer's* World *sold five million papers a week.*

V-7 *Of course artists in Madrid's* Don Quijote *and* Blanco y Negro *and Barcelona's* El Nacional *were equally busy drumming up hatred of the United States. Many of their cartoons were based on the Yankee Pig theme.*

V-8 *One of the rare American cartoonists to oppose the war was William H. Walker of* Life; *seventeen years later, however, he would be a strong interventionist when war broke out in Europe.*

123

ery, Frederick Burr Opper has never had an equal.

Opper had spent eighteen years with *Puck* before joining the New York *Journal;* he would remain with the Hearst organization for thirty-two years, until failing eyesight forced his retirement in 1932. ("I could no longer see the point of my cartoons," he said.) His long and continually fruitful career was a major exception to the cartoonists' frequent pattern of declining creativity; indeed, his early work was highly imitative of Keppler, and *Puck*'s huge lithographic canvasses were ill-suited to his talents. It was only when he turned to smaller pen and ink drawings that his own style emerged—a style, wrote Thomas Craven, that was "a mixture of barbed wire and chicken scratches."[2]

Most memorable of Opper's cartoons were the series that he strung out through 1900, 1901, 1902, and 1903— notably "Willie and His Papa," "The M'Kinley Minstrels," "An Alphabet of Joyous Trusts," "Alice in Plunderland," "Popular Pictures For the People," and "Popular Songs." The artist loved to repeat a theme day after day, the repetition having the effect of heightening the wit so that the whole was greater than the sum of its parts.

For many cartoonists the transition from magazines to newspapers was difficult, often impossible. The leisurely routine of the weekly journals was replaced by a grinding, daily demand:

V-9 *The continuing exploits of Willie (McKinley) and Teddy (Roosevelt) were eagerly awaited in the Roosevelt household, the Rough Rider told W. A. Rogers, and "his children got no end of amusement out of them, too."*

many artists quickly found they could not stand the pace or the increased drain on their creative juices. Moreover, the different media required different techniques. In terms of both the artist's time and the lack of sophistication of newspaper reproduction, it was impossible to use the intricate group scenes that had been the staple of *Puck*

THE M'KINLEY MINSTRELS.
(Copyright, 190x by W. R. Hearst.)

"We will now give a benefit for our esteemed fellow citizen, Andy Carnegie, who is retiring from business with a modest competence. Our talented End Men will do a Double Clog Dance, while the entire Company will give their matchless Character Impersonations, and sing a glee that goes like this:
"'We're a jolly lot of Actors, and we give a rattling play,
And whether they like the show or not, we make the Public pay.'"

V-10   *Another variation of the theme was Opper's series "The Little Boy and The Big Boys." The Little Boy was his famous symbol, The Common People (see I-33); The Big Boys, of course, were various trusts.*

Nursery Rhymes for Infant Industries.
An Alphabet of Joyous Trusts—No. 5.
COPYRIGHT, 1902, BY W. R. HEARST.

E   'S the Electric Trust. Quick as a flash
He turns on his current and shocks out your cash!

IS IT STRONG ENOUGH FOR YOU?

V-11   *At the end of this series Opper wrote: "With these alphabet pictures the artist took pains,/ But he's got to stop now, and with grief nearly busts/ 'Cause our language but twenty-six letters contains,/ Though our country contains twenty-six hundred Trusts."*

and *Judge.* Opper was one of the few men to make the changeover comfortably. Most of the newspapers would be serviced by a new breed of cartoonist.

Now instead of a handful of magazines, most of them headquartered in New York, literally hundreds of newspapers all over the country had need of political cartoonists. Although the best

of these artists were sometimes lured to the New York dailies, a number of other regions developed and retained outstanding talent. At the turn of the century Minnesota's Twin Cities had a particularly rich vein of cartooning resources with Charles L. (Bart) Bartholomew of the Minneapolis *Journal*, R. C. (Doc) Bowman of the Minneapolis

Tribune, and G. W. Rehse of the St. Paul *Pioneer Press.* Right from the beginning of the newspaper period Chicago has been the outstanding city for stockpiling capable cartoonists. Over the years such early Chicago leaders as Charles Lederer, T. E. Powers, Art Young, and J. Campbell Cory have been succeeded by Luther Bradley, Vaughn Shoemaker, Jacob Burck, Bill Mauldin, John Fischetti, and, on the Chicago *Tribune* (once called "a kind of Yellowstone Park for the disappearing herd of cartoonists"), John T. McCutcheon, Carey Orr, and Joseph Parrish. This geographical diversity is a noteworthy phenomenon. William A. Ireland, a first-ranked cartoonist on the Columbus (Ohio) *Dispatch* for many years, constantly refused offers from papers in greater metropolitan areas. He explained, "My object isn't to break into New York; it is to break back to Chillicothe."

The first of the major figures to come of age in newspaper cartooning was Homer Davenport. He and Opper became Hearst's one-two punch. But, unlike the gentle Opper's, Davenport's "pictures invite battle and tears," wrote editor Horace Traubel.[3] Davenport was a bruiser whose best blow was a roundhouse to the midsection.

Born in Silverton, Oregon, fifteen miles east of Salem, Homer Davenport was to play the role of "country boy" even after he became New York's highest-paid cartoonist. "The funniest

V-12 *"Hanna's eyes are inclined to be small and keen . . . and without detracting any from his character of face the artist can draw them much smaller. . . . His nose is short and very stout at the base, and with a rise at the point. This also can be nicely exaggerated. Next [his] ears, which are the most prominent of any of his features; his ear's are as big and as shapely as well developed pie plant leaves. Any old thing you car to draw, if it has room on the paper, will do for Hanna's ears and at the same time add to your picture of Hanna. In general make-up [Hanna], while a rather competent-looking business man, has a coarse appearance, and to make him a little coarser helps the cartoon, which is, in brief, merely an exaggeration of certain truths"—Homer Davenport, 1899.*

MARK HANNA AS HE IS AND AS DAVENPORT MADE HIM.

When Hanna and Davenport finally met after the 1896 election, the politician supposedly said, "I admire your execution but damn your conception." Davenport recorded the meeting with these sketches.

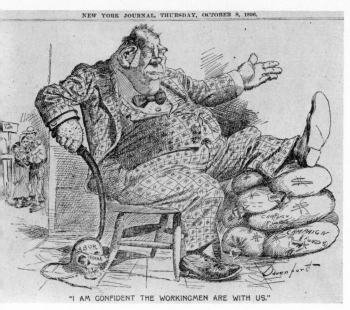

"I AM CONFIDENT THE WORKINGMEN ARE WITH US."

V-13 During the 1896 campaign Hanna showed a Davenport cartoon to Senator Nathan B. Scott of West Virginia. "That hurts . . . to be held up to the gaze of the world as a murderer of women and children," said Hanna. "I tell you it hurts." Tears ran down Hanna's cheeks; he turned and silently walked away. Later the New York Journal quoted Hanna as saying, "That fellow Davenport drew a cartoon of me with my feet on the skull bones of labor, and giving me the most brutal face that he could draw. That was a picture for which the man who drew it ought to have been sent to the penitentiary."

A MAN OF MARK!

THE NEW ANTHEM AT PHILADELPHIA.

Ring Out and Proclaim Trust-Imperialism Throughout the Land.

V-14 McKinley always appeared in Davenport's 1896 cartoons as Hanna's puppet or dupe. The cartoonist had never seen Hanna, but editor Murat Halstead took him to meet the candidate, a move that was credited with the less vitriolic treatment McKinley received.

Hanna was really an enlightened employer who had said of George Pullman's refusal to arbitrate the railroad strike of 1894: "A man who won't meet his men half-way is a God-damn fool!" Yet Davenport so popularized another view of Hanna that when, during a campaign speech, he offered $100 to find a dollar mark on his suit, a man shouted: "Of course we can't see 'em. They're branded on yer hide."

V-15 Beside his Mark Hanna, a major creation of Davenport's was a huge barbarian with a sort of Assyrian beard. This figure, labeled "The Trust," had a considerable vogue, but its longevity was severely limited because it was so foreign to the American scene and because, in the hands of other artists, it became commonplace and lost its raw power.

TO CYCLERS!!
READ TO-MORROW'S
JOURNAL FOR SOMETHING
THAT WILL INTEREST YOU.

NEW YORK JOURNAL

WHEELWOMEN!!
YOU MUST NOT FAIL TO
READ THE JOURNAL TO-
MORROW. DON'T MISS IT!

NO. 5,038.   NEW YORK, TUESDAY, SEPTEMBER 1, 1896.—12 PAGES.—COPYRIGHT, 1896, BY W. R. HEARST   PRICE ONE CENT.

BRYAN GREETED IN M'KINLEY'S STATE.

Democratic Candidate Given an Enthusiastic Welcome.

A Hundred Thousand Cheering Voters Turn Out in Cleveland.

Part of the Crowd Hails from Canton and Other Near-by Towns.

Three Speeches Received with Demonstration Never Before Equalled in the Forest City.

NOMINEE'S FAREWELL TO NEW YORK.

Tells the People That They Should Control the Buffalo Convention—Can Be Done by Giving Instructions to Delegates.

(Continued on Third Page.)

WILD SPOTTED BEAST ATE UP STRAY DOGS.

Had Escaped from a Circus and Was Thought to Be a Bengal Tiger.

Summer Residents Terrorized and Old Long Island Farmers on the Hunt.

Some Thought He Was a Leopard, but All Agreed He Could Rapidly Change His Spots.

WAS SHOT AT LAST IN A TREE.

Perhaps the Beast Might Still Be Roaming and Devouring Had He Not Rolled in a Poor Colored Man's Tater Patch.

VERMONT NAMES A GOVERNOR TO-DAY.

Senator Morrill Claims the State for Republicans by 35,000.

Democrats Only Hope to Reduce the Majority to 15,000.

Farmers Will Vote for Silver, and Sticknyites May Not Support Josiah Grout.

FIERCE CAMPAIGN OF EDUCATION.

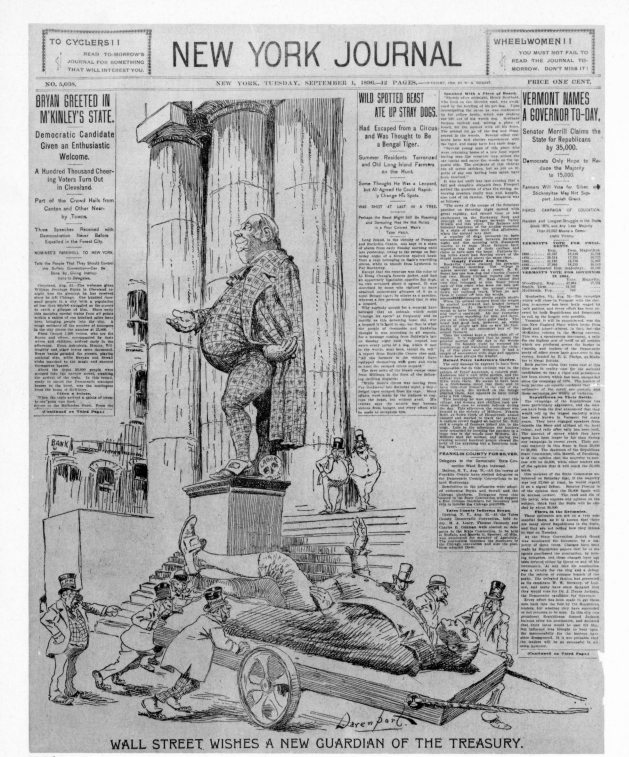

WALL STREET WISHES A NEW GUARDIAN OF THE TREASURY.

Darenport.

V-16

things happen to me," he said. "I am always being taken for my coachman, or a groom in my stable, or some sort of a servant."[4] Some imagined that there must be a silent partner behind the powerful Nastian creations that he turned out for the *Journal*, but those who were not misled by the hayseed pose discovered that Davenport was a shrewd operator who once even out-maneuvered a Bedouin chieftain in a horse trade.[5]

Davenport was Hearst's only "home-grown" cartoonist; he had first employed the artist on his San Francisco *Examiner* and brought him east in time for the 1896 Presidential campaign, during which Hearst was the one major publisher in the country to support Democrat William Jennings Bryan, and Davenport was to invent an image of Republican campaign manager Mark

Hanna that would haunt the Cleveland industrialist for the rest of his life.

There was one phenomenon that Opper, Davenport, and the other turn-of-the-century artists could always count on to make their lives easier—Theodore Roosevelt. The Rough Rider President was, in the words of John T. McCutcheon, "an inexhaustible Golconda of inspiration for the cartoonist."[6] He was himself a frustrated cartoonist (as seen from the sketches with which he peppered his delightful letters to his children), and he rarely took offense at even the most outrageous crimes that the cartooning fraternity perpetrated against his features.[7] In fact, sportsman Roosevelt was known to have been publicly irritated by just one cartoon (in the Wichita *Eagle*), and then only

V-17   *"The Head of the Procession Coming Out of Wall Street."*
   When asked about his inspiration for "The Trust" figure, Davenport said, "As a matter of fact, I got the idea in St. Mark's Square in Venice. Seeing a flock of pigeons flying about in that neighborhood I immediately, with my love of birds and beasts, determined by *fair means or foul to purloin a pair. I watched them fly hither and thither, and in following them came across a statue of Samson throwing some man or other— I forget his name—to the ground. The abnormal size of the muscles of the figure struck me at once, and turning round to my wife, who was with me, I said with a sudden inspired thought, 'The Trusts!' "*

WHAT MAY HAPPEN TO TEDDY IF HE DOESN'T STOP MAKING SPEECHES ABOUT HIMSELF.

V-19

V-20

We Wouldn't Say "Blockhead"

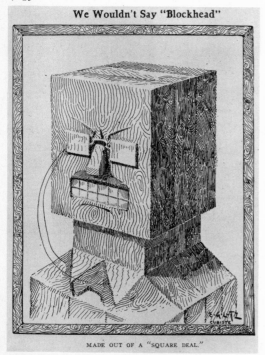

MADE OUT OF A "SQUARE DEAL."

TEMPLE DE TRUTH

President Roosevelt and the Third Term Nomination---Is This a Prophecy?

V-21

V-18, V-19, V-20, V-21   *Teddy Roosevelt had the sort of face that could make even the most inept cartoonist into a master for the moment. He could be effortlessly transformed into a gargoyle or a block of wood, the letter "I," or the White House. The dentist, he said, is easier on my teeth than are the cartoonists. Yet he collected their drawings of him, and as President he hung over his desk an 1884 Puck cartoon that claimed he was not qualified for higher office.*

130

V-22 *"In the 50 years since caricature became a feature of American journalism, no man has been the subject of so many cartoons as [Theodore] Roosevelt"* —Art Young, 1939.

V-23 *During a Mississippi bear hunt in 1902 President Roosevelt refused to shoot a cub and inspired Clifford Berryman of the Washington* Post *to invent the "Teddy Bear." Berryman's little bear became his "dingbat"—the symbol (often an animal) that many artists repeat in all their cartoons as a trademark.*

because it showed him mounting a "war horse" with the wrong foot in the stirrup!

Besides having the famous teeth and moustache, the penchant for costumes, and the talent for self-dramatization, Roosevelt was a master wordsmith whose ability to invent phrases like "my hat's in the ring," "rough riders," "speak softly and carry a big stick," "muckrackers," "I feel like a bull moose," would provide the cartoonists with a steady diet of new symbols. It is hardly surprising that many of the outstanding cartoonists of the era—Davenport, Opper, the younger Keppler, Berryman, McCutcheon, Darling—found in Roosevelt the inspiration for their best-known work.

DRAWING THE LINE IN MISSISSIPPI

V-24 *Homer Davenport's best-known cartoon, although expressionless and humorless, is an extremely effective campaign document, for the point is unmistakable: Uncle Sam stands behind T. R. The Republicans supposedly spent $200,000 printing and circulating the drawing before the 1904 election.*

UNCLE SAM. *"After all is said and done, he's still 'Good Enough for Me.'*

V-25 *As well as having a little fun at Davenport's expense, Charles Macauley of the New York* World *also earned a place in T. R. lore by creating the "Big Stick" as a cartoon symbol.*

"HE'S GOOD ENOUGH FOR ME."

V-26 *In this 1907* Puck *cartoon, the most famous by Joseph Keppler, Jr., there is an obvious similarity of style between father and son, although of the two the younger Keppler chose much simpler designs, used fewer figures, and was more apt to exaggerate features. Keppler, Jr., left cartooning after he sold* Puck *in 1914 and devoted the remaining forty-two years of his life to improving the conditions of the American Indians.*

THE COURTSHIP OF BILL TAFT.

V-27 *The peripatetic Teddy was the ideal subject for John T. McCutcheon. The artist paid little attention to the rules of perspective but contrived to fill his pictures with large crowds and lots of amusing action. He sometimes spent six or eight hours drawing a cartoon.*

"I always enjoyed drawing a type of cartoon which might be considered a sort of pictorial breakfast food. It had the cardinal asset of making the beginning of a day sunnier. It is safe to say the prairies were not set afire by these cartoons, yet they had the merit of offending no one. Their excuse lay in the belief that a happy man is capable of a more constructive day's work than a glum one"—John T. McCutcheon.

THE PRESIDENTIAL HOLIDAY

HE ARRIVES IN "SAN ANTONE" TO ATTEND A REUNION OF THE ROUGH RIDERS.

THE MYSTERIOUS STRANGER.

V-28 *When the Republican Roosevelt carried Democratic Missouri in 1904, McCutcheon commemorated the event in what was to become his best-known political cartoon. It took the artist less than a half hour to draw, and the title was added by the Chicago Tribune's managing editor.*

"THE LONG, LONG TRAIL"

V-29, V-30 *Jay N. (Ding)
Darling's tribute to T. R. upon his
death in 1919 was hurriedly drawn
and repeated an idea the artist had
used two years before to eulogize
Buffalo Bill Cody (above). "Ding"
meant the Roosevelt cartoon only
for the first edition of his newspaper
(after which he would replace it with
a more formal design), but the
drawing was an instant success and
now may be the most reproduced
cartoon of the much-cartooned
Rough Rider.*

If the "Cartoon Trust" desired a Democratic counterpart to Theodore Roosevelt, the logical choice would have been Woodrow Wilson. But the stern schoolmaster in politics interested the cartoonists relatively little; rather, it was William Jennings Bryan who captured their imagination.

Bryan's quest for the Presidency became a recurring theme for a generation of writers and artists. The record they left forms a sort of political "seven ages of man" as they traced his evolution from the handsome thirty-six-year-old "Boy Orator of the Platte" who swept the 1896 Democratic convention to the bloated, balding old man who opposed the teaching of the Darwinian theory at the famous Scopes trial of 1925.

V-31

134

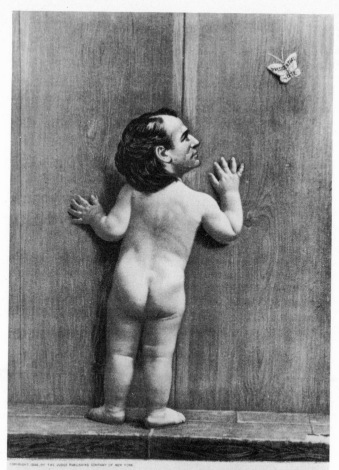

LITTLE BILLY BRYAN CHASING BUTTERFLIES.

V-32 **1896** *The youngest man to run for President is spoofed by adding his face to a popular "cabinet photograph."*

V-33 **1900** *During his second Presidential campaign Bryan continued to press for the coinage of silver at a ratio of 16–1, a stand that united even such bitter rivals as* Puck *and* Judge *in opposition to him.*

"TRADE FOLLOWS THE FLAG," BUT DEMOCRATS FOLLOW THE FOOL.

TEMPTATION

V-34 1904 *Bryan resisted the "temptation" to a direct confrontation with Teddy Roosevelt and left the undesired nomination to Alton B. Parker, a little-known New York judge.*

V-35 1908 *But he came back four years later to become the only person ever to receive three major party nominations for President.*

SUNSHINE---AND SHADOW

ANOTHER FAREWELL TOUR?

V-36 1912 *Heavier and balder, still the perennial optimist—yet the delegates to the Democratic presidential convention preferred Gov. Woodrow Wilson of New Jersey.*

Dropping the pilot.

ORANG-UTANS
HABITAT—AFRICA

GATHERING DATA FOR THE TENNESSEE TRIAL

V-37 1915 (TOP) *His tour as Wilson's Secretary of State was cut short when his deeply held pacifism forced his resignation.*

V-38 1925 *The last public act of the once "Peerless Leader" was to prosecute a schoolteacher for teaching evolution. William Jennings Bryan died five days after the trial ended.*

The prelude to the Spanish-American War had proved once more that the editorial cartoonists could bring a heated situation to a boil. Again in the 1914–17 period, as the nation watched war spread over the European continent, the cartoonists were actively propagandizing for American intervention on the side of the English and French. Led by William A. Rogers of the *Herald*, the artists on the New York papers were especially outspoken. A steady stream of anti-German cartoons flowed from Nelson Harding, Brooklyn *Eagle;* Robert Carter, *Evening Sun;* Edwin Marcus, *Times;* Sid Greene, *Evening Telegram;* J. H. Cassell, *Evening World;* and, somewhat later than the others, Rollin Kirby of the *World.* Of all the cartoonists on major U.S. dailies, only Luther D. Bradley of the Chicago *Daily News* opposed American military involvement. Not that Bradley was pro-German; rather he maintained a scrupulous neutrality, condemning only war and barbarism. But Bradley died on January 9, 1917, and it will never be known if he could have held out against the rising demands for war that swept the country.

Clearly the most significant cartoonist in the American press during the war was not an American at all but a Dutchman, Louis Raemaekers, whose work originally appeared in the Amsterdam *Telegraaf.* Before the war was

HE HAD EXPECTED TO FIND THE PRESIDENT ALONE.

V-39

ANOTHER CASE OF WIPING HANDS ON THE AMERICAN FLAG.

V-41

WHAT WE'RE GOING TO DO TO THOSE NEUTRALS WILL BREAK OUR TENDER HEARTS.

V-40

V-39, V-40, V-41   *"You can no more give all sides of a question in a cartoon than you can draw all sides of a house in a picture,"* wrote William A. Rogers of the New York Herald, *whose pro-war cartoons earned him the French Legion of Honor. Rogers earlier had done important work in exposing municipal and state corruption for* Harper's Weekly, *but his drawings had a certain reserve that kept him from entering the Nast–Davenport class.*

OPPOSITE PAGE   V-42, V-43, V-44   *Luther Bradley had a strange career in that, after tours at Yale and with his father's real estate business, he left on an around-the-world cruise and, having a long layover in Australia, tried his hand at cartooning, a profession for which he had no training. He remained in Australia for eleven years, most of the time with the Melbourne* Punch, *before returning to Chicago, where he joined the staff of the* Daily News *in 1899. "The Final Answer?" was his last cartoon, published five days before his death.*

OUT?

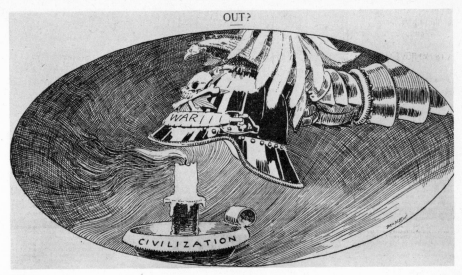

V-42

JUST FOR GOOD MEASURE.

V-43

V-44

THE FINAL ANSWER?

over, the German government had put a price on his head, the Dutch government had prosecuted him for endangering its neutrality (he was acquitted), and there was even a report that the Germans had attempted to torpedo the ship on which he left Holland for exile in England. Raemaekers' pictures often combined a haunting beauty with a biting satire. In the United States his cartoons were widely reproduced through an uneasy agreement between the artist and William Randolph Hearst.

For most American cartoonists, however, the coming of war meant that patriotism replaced originality, and their role, as they saw it, became little more than government cheerleader. (A notable exception was Oscar Cesare of the New York *Sun* and later the New York *Evening Post,* a Swedish-born artist who had married O. Henry's daughter.)[8]

In December, 1917, a young man named George J. Hecht (later the founder of *Parents' Magazine* and *True Comics*) set up a Bureau of Cartoons in Washington under the auspices of the National Committee of Patriotic Societies. Its purpose was to mobilize the cartoonists for the war effort. By the following June, Hecht's operation was incorporated into the government. The Bureau published a weekly *Bulletin for Cartoonists,* which listed fitting subjects and often came close to providing the pictorial ideas themselves.

KULTUR HAS PASSED HERE

V-45   *"I have explored a hell, and it was terror unspeakable"—Louis Raemaekers.*

For example, the first *Bulletin* was devoted to Red Cross themes and the suggestions included:

USELESS CHRISTMAS PRESENTS VS. RED CROSS MEMBERSHIPS—Showing that a Red Cross membership is better than embroidered slippers or a string of beads.

THE RED CROSS VS. THE IRON CROSS. Would you not rather wear a Red Cross than an iron cross of autocracy and slavery? Only a heart and a dollar are required.

"The purpose of the Bulletin [for Cartoonists] was distinctly not to give directions. The suggestions that were offered were to enable cartoonists to be of the greatest possible service. In this way a considerable cartoon power was developed which helped the Government in stimulating recruiting, popularizing the draft, saving food and fuel, selling Liberty Bonds and War Savings Stamps, warning against German propaganda and in solving a myriad of other difficult war problems"—George Hecht, 1919.

V-47   *"The Cornerstone."*

V-46   *"We Can, We Must, and We Will!"*

V-48   *"The Sweetheart of the Allies!"*

Yet one group of American cartoonists took a consistently pacifist position even after the U.S. had entered the war. Their opinions appeared in journals of minuscule circulation, and their influence on the masses was virtually nil. As artists, however, they were doing work that was generally well above the caliber seen in the popular press, and stylistically their influence is still being felt in the cartooning profession.

These were the radicals. Some called themselves anarchists. Most were Socialists.

Their primary showcase was *The Masses* (1911–17), a handsome Green-wich Village magazine whose circulation averaged 12,000.[9] (In 1905, B. O. Flower wrote that in all of America there was only one Socialist drawing cartoons—Ryan Walker of *Appeal to Reason*, a Girard, Kansas, publication.)[10] The first art editor of *The Masses* was John Sloan, who had also been a Socialist party candidate for the New York legislature in 1910 at which time he received 102 votes. (See I-8.) He recruited such talent as George Bellows and Stuart Davis, but while their art was rich in social content it was more illustration than cartoon, and they were unhappy that the editors

EUROPE, 1916

V-49   *Boardman Robinson, a picturesque figure with a reddish beard, was the son of a Nova Scotia sea captain. He drew cartoons for the conservative New York* Tribune *(1910–14) until he threw over this high-paying job to go to Russia with John Reed for the Socialist-oriented* Metropolitan Magazine *(financed by multimillionaire Harry Payne Whitney).*

Robinson's style was an attempt to adapt the lithographic power of Daumier to the photoengraving process by drawing with a crayon on grained paper. This created a palpitating effect that immediately influenced Robert Minor, Rollin Kirby, Clive Weed, and Oscar Cesare, among others. Later, as teacher at the Art Students' League in New York (1919–30), Robinson would influence another generation of cartoonists.

were attempting to make them into cartoonists by tagging captions onto their work.[11]

In *The Masses* group, however, were three men who were proud to be labeled cartoonists—Boardman Robinson, Robert Minor, and Art Young.

The belligerent antiwar posture of *The Masses* led to its suppression by the U.S. Government in 1917. When Art Young, along with other editors, was brought to trial under the Espion-age Act, he seemed singularly uninterested in the proceedings and even, on one occasion, managed to fall asleep in the courtroom. (Two trials ended in hung juries.) *The Masses* was superseded by *The Liberator* in 1918, which, in turn, was merged into *The Worker's Monthly* in 1924, with *The New Masses* making its first appearance in 1926. As the radical left became more and more communistic and doctrinaire, the quality of its humor degenerated into

SYSTEM

V-50 *"When I use a large, blunt crayon it is not for the sake of the appearance of the lines, but because it forces simplicity—for you cannot draw tedious detail with a big crayon,"* wrote Robert Minor, who might have been the outstanding American cartoonist of the twentieth century if he had not instead chosen to become "Fighting Bob," Communist party candidate for Governor of New York (1932), Mayor of New York City (1933), and U.S. Senator (1936); editor of the Daily Worker; and Acting Secretary General of the Communist party in the United States after Earl Browder was jailed in 1941.

V-51 *Art Young, a product of the Middle West who had begun his career on the* Chicago *Inter-Ocean in 1884, was the mainstay of the cartooning staff of* The Masses. *His unique style suggested to Heywood Broun that he must have been "frightened by a woodcut in his early life." Few of Young's cartoons were related to topical issues; rather, he noted, "practically all of them are generalizations on the one important issue of this era the world over: Plutocracy versus the principles of Socialism. . . ."*

One of the few bright spots in left-wing journalism during the postwar period was Good Morning (subtitle: The Weekly Burst of Humor, Satire and Fun), *which appeared from 1919 through 1921 under Young's jovial management.*

heavy-handed propaganda, although throughout the 1920s and '30s some effective work was still being done by Fred Ellis, Jacob Burck, Maurice Becker, William Gropper, and Clive Weed.[12]

In the wake of World War I the nation passed two Constitutional amendments. One outlawed the sale or manufacture of intoxicating liquors; the other granted women the right to vote. The Eighteenth and Nineteenth Amendments, coming on the heels of each other in 1919 and 1920, were not entirely unconnected. Behind both could be seen the Woman's Christian Temperance Union, the reformist urge, wartime pressures, the feeling that women as voters would be an anti-alcohol force—and the cartoonists. For prohibition and woman suffrage were, in the opinion of America's cartoonists, the two most satire-provoking, gag-producing issues that had ever come along to rescue a harried artist from an impending deadline.

DECORATING THE GREATEST HERO

V-52   *A* Good Morning *cartoon by William Gropper, whose artistry triggered an international incident in 1935 when a tongue-in-cheek drawing entitled "Japan's Emperor Gets the Nobel Peace Prize" was run in* Vanity Fair. *The magazine was banned in Japan, where a Foreign Office spokesman stated, "The cartoon is regarded as insulting to the Japanese Emperor." Gropper replied, "The whole business seems to me to be the height of divine stupidity."*

SOCIETY NOTE FROM MOSCOW

Count Parasitsky will not occupy his palatial residence in the mountains this summer. He expects to remain in the city and do uplift work.

V-53   Good Morning *took a view of the Russian Revolution somewhat different from that of the average American journal. "Society Note" was a series by Al Frueh, whose brilliant caricatures of theatrical figures was a feature of the New York* World *and who would later become a star of* The New Yorker.

V-54 *Woman suffrage was hardly a new concern in the twentieth century. Back in 1647 Mistress Margaret Brent asked for "place and voyce" in the Maryland legislature. At the Woman's Rights Convention, held at Seneca Falls, New York, in 1848, a resolution formally demanded the ballot for females, and in 1869, when C. G. Bush drew this cartoon for* Harper's Weekly, *the Territory of Wyoming granted unrestricted suffrage for women.*

Gen. Rosalie Jones crossing the Delaware.

V-55

V-55, V-56, V-57, V-58
James Donahey of the Cleveland Plain Dealer *may have seen the suffragists in the role of Washington and his heroic troops crossing the Delaware, but most*

cartoonists—males all—made fun of the ladies' pretensions. It was the one issue on which Joseph Keppler, Sr., was known to have altered his views. In 1870 the great cartoonist was all for women's voting, but the next year he opposed the idea. His biographer, Draper Hill, commented, "It is assumed that his marriage in July of 1870 is an event of complete irrelevance in this respect." However, the male politician, as John Knott of the Dallas News points out in his Adams and Eve cartoon, saw a new beauty in the fair sex after the passage of the Nineteenth Amendment.

V-56

THE ONLY WAY.

Specker—"The only way we can gain woman's suffrage is by making our appeal through our charm, our grace, and our bea...

"TOUCH ME NOT, I'M A LADY!"

V-57

THE TWO ADAMS: "IT WAS MY RIB, EVE"

POLITICAL GARDEN OF EDEN

WOMAN SUFFRAGE

G.O.P.

DEM

V-58

146

The prohibition movement was a venerable institution by the time the federal government entered the picture. The American Temperance Society was formed in 1826; the National Prohibition Party came along in 1869 and fielded its first Presidential ticket three years later. Maine abolished the sale of liquor in 1846, and Vermont and New Hampshire passed "Maine Laws" in 1852 and 1855, respectively.

The 1920s, the decade that was personified by John Held, Jr.'s impish flapper, that advertised itself as gay and

V-59

Even Rollin Kirby's famous Mr. Dry (below), which came to represent the Prohibition Era, had nineteenth-century antecedents in Joseph Keppler's Old Man Prohibition (shown above in an 1889 cartoon but actually invented by Keppler in 1869). Moreover, a similar figure was used by mid-nineteenth-century artists to depict William Lloyd Garrison and the ultra-Abolitionists.

V-60

"NOW, THEN, ALL TOGETHER: 'MY COUNTRY, 'TIS OF THEE!'"

147

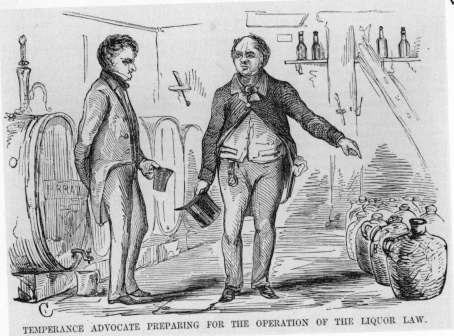

TEMPERANCE ADVOCATE PREPARING FOR THE OPERATION OF THE LIQUOR LAW.

V-61, V-62 *As the cartoonists viewed Prohibition, 1852–55. . . .*

Novel Effects of the Prohibition.

Independent American Citizen, (loq.)—(hic)—WHAT A LUXURY A
GOOD GLASS OF GROG IS! I NEVER (hic) DRANK MUCH BEFORE THEY
PASSED A LIQUOR LAW. BUT NOW (hic) I GO IT, OUT O' SPITE. BLOWED
IF I DONT MAKE A REGULAR (hic) BRANDY PEACH OF MYSELF.

V-63

The Prohibitionist Finds a Horrid Old Dandelion on His Estate and Walks Half a Mile to Burn It in the Kitchen Stove—*By Webster*

V-63, V-64 *. . . As the cartoonists still viewed Prohibition, 1919–33.*

V-64

roaring, ended with a crash. The night-mare collapse of the stock market on November 13, 1929, ushered in the Great Depression. Herbert Hoover, the hapless President, claimed prosperity was just around the corner, but the statistics made hollow his prediction: one out of four farms were sold for taxes, 5000 banks were closed, and, by 1933, there were 15 million unemployed Americans.

In 1933 there was also a new President, Franklin D. Roosevelt. He called his Administration the New Deal, and its programs exploded over the American landscape like a string of alphabetic firecrackers—CCC, AAA, NRA, WPA, TVA. The President lashed out at the Depression in all directions, and the people rewarded his effort in 1936 by giving him the greatest electoral victory of modern times.

The finest appreciation in cartoons of what Franklin Roosevelt was attempting to do—if only by picturing his

V-65, V-66 A few major cartoonists gave powerful support to the New Deal, such as Fitzpatrick of the St. Louis Post-Dispatch *and Batchelor of the New York* Daily News. *(Ironically, the latter was to become cartoonist for the ultra-conservative* National Review.) *Others sympathetic to Roosevelt were Harold Talburt of the Scripps-Howard chain and, at first, the Chicago* Tribune's *John T. McCutcheon, who refused to give aid to his publisher, Robert McCormick. (Earlier, McCutcheon had also opposed his publisher's anti-Prohibition stand.)*

ONE PERSON OUT OF EVERY TEN
—*WPA Administrator Hopkins.*

V-65

"Yes, You Remembered Me"

V-66

V-67, V-68 *But the great majority of
cartoonists—perhaps reflecting the great
majority of their publishers—were hostile
to the New Deal. The work of Herbert
Johnson, Saturday Evening Post,
and Jay N. (Ding) Darling, New York
Herald Tribune, is representative of their
viewpoint during the 1930's. The
Washington Star's Cliff Berryman in 1938
showed the American farmers
goosestepping before "Fuehrer"
Henry Wallace, the Secretary of
Agriculture. Never had cartoonists and
public opinion been on such separate
tracks, and never had each so little effect
on the other.
Darling's "Halloween 1936"—showing
Harry Hopkins, James Farley, and F.D.R.
as young pranksters—was drawn for the
private amusement of his co-workers, but
Mrs. Ogden Reid, wife of the publisher,
is said to have told the editors: "If you don't
publish it, I'll put it on the woman's page!"*

V-68

effect on the "upper class"—came not from the newspapers but from an unexpected source, a new magazine that at first tried hard to stay out of politics. Since the golden days of *Puck, Judge,* and *Life,* the humor magazines had been having rough sledding. In 1917 *Puck* was taken over by Hearst, who killed it the next year and transplanted the famous *Puck* trademark onto the masthead of his Sunday comic supplement. By 1920 *Judge* had stooped to soliciting "Krazy Kracks" at five dollars a crack and printed "Funnybones" stories in bone-shaped boxes. *Life* had been taken over by Charles Dana Gibson, a better artist than publisher, and was limping along with cartoons left over from the era of the two-line caption and the "he–she" joke.

Then, in 1925, *The New Yorker,* whose prospectus announced that it

"And if Roosevelt is not reëlected, perhaps even a villa in Newport, my dearest sweet."

V-69   The New Yorker's best years coincided with the Depression, and although its cartoons were mainly of the social genre, hardly an issue appeared without one that was intrinsically political. A dowager might declare: "We can't simply dismiss the talk of revolution, my dear. This morning Burke neglected to touch his cap." Or one of Peter Arno's representatives of the upper crust says, "Come on—we're going to the Trans-Lux and hiss Roosevelt."

V-70   In another famous New Yorker cartoon (by Alan Dunn in 1941), a sergeant addresses his troops: "And hereafter if there is anything you don't like, come to me—don't write to Mrs. Roosevelt." The President's peripatetic wife, however, was not known to have held cartoonists in particular high regard and reportedly once said she could never forgive "Ding" for depicting her husband as Little Lord Fauntleroy.

"For gosh sakes, here comes Mrs. Roosevelt!"

V-71

The Sphinx Speaks, but Says Nothing

V-71, V-72 *Franklin Roosevelt, like his fifth cousin, Theodore, was generally amused by the cartoonists. Shortly after his death in 1945,* The New Republic *declared that the cartoons shown above and below had been his favorites by American artists. (He was also partial to the work of Colonel Blimp's creator, David Low, according to the magazine.) F.D.R. took special delight in a cartoon that poked fun at a Republican effort to make his dog Fala into a campaign issue during the 1944 election.*

V-72

would be designed for the sophisticate rather than "the old lady of Dubuque," was founded by Harold Ross, a high school dropout and tramp newspaperman who had learned the rudiments of editing on *Stars and Stripes* during the World War. Part of Ross' genius, as his friend James Thurber explained, was a "major gift of surrounding himself with some of the best talent in America, despite his own literary and artistic limitations." One of his first catches was art director Rea Irvin, and soon the accepted way to read *The New Yorker* was by starting with the cartoons.[13]

Yet, ironically, it was not Franklin Delano Roosevelt, the only four-term President of the United States, who most captured the cartoonists' imagination during the New Deal era but a gentleman with a healthy dislike of the President: a coal miner's son, who had worked in the mines as a boy and somehow had acquired a thorough knowledge of the works of Shakespeare and the King James' Bible, from which he quoted in the deepest bass voice outside of the Metropolitan Opera.

He was the President of the United Mine Workers and the founder of the Congress of Industrial Organizations. Nineteenth-century cartoonists had had their Ben Butler, Tom Reed, and Roscoe Conkling, but, as Gerald Johnson pointed out, "John Llewellyn Lewis was without doubt one of God's greatest

V-73

V-73, V-74, V-75, V-76
"People frequently comment that faces like [John L.] Lewis' must be easy to do, and for a quick recognizable cartoon likeness they are. But there is such a thing as a face being almost too easy—or having too many prominent characteristics. Lewis' distinctinctive visage defies the cartoonist to improve on a caricature already well done. All the features scream for attention."—Herblock.

V-74

V-75

V-76

gifts to American cartoonists in the twentieth century. His physical appearance made him easy to caricature and his salient personality constantly brought him into situations lending themselves to satire. It is not that Mr. Lewis was ever a comic character, but that he was masterful, and a truly masterful man is always running into situations in which there is an element of comedy."[14]

The 1930s also witnessed the rise of Hitlerism in Europe, and most American cartoonists (like the majority of the people for whom they drew) felt neither overly concerned nor personally threatened. Rather than portray Hit-

ler as the terrifying would-be conqueror that he was, they were more apt to pictorially turn him into a comic figure—mountebank, village idiot, or just that little man with the funny mustache.

Two cartoonists in the Middle West, historically the home of American isolationism, took the lead in trying to explain the menace of events across the Atlantic. They were very different in style and politics. Daniel R. Fitzpatrick of the St. Louis *Post-Dispatch* usually sided with liberal Democrats. Vaughn Shoemaker of the Chicago *Daily News* usually sided with conservative Republicans. Fitzpatrick employed a powerful crayon-on-grained-paper technique that

"Come on in, I'll treat you right. I used to know your daddy."

V-77 *The prevailing view of the coming of the war as a vice (prostitution), which appealed to the hedonistic appetite of the European—and, by implication, was something from which the moralistic American could abstain—was brilliantly presented by C. D. Batchelor of the New York* Daily News *in a cartoon that won the Pulitzer Prize in 1937. This prestigious award had been given since 1922, usually to the right person for the wrong reason; by and large, the judges honored those drawings that avoided the specific and the controversial. But Batchelor's design has a power that recalls John Leech's classic of the Crimean War, "General Février Turned Traitor," in which the Russian winter is also pictured with a death's-head.*

155

Swastika Over Germany

V-78

POLAND

NEXT!

V-79

V-78, V-79 *"How to portray the new movement in cartoon language? Perhaps this is a good example of the distilling process a cartoonist indulges in. The swastika, emblem of the movement, was modified to depict the real nature of Nazism. It is pure pictorial language and as simple as a drawing by an early cave man. . . .*

"Later, I transformed the swastika into a huge, tumbling engine of destruction which I used on a number of occasions"
—D. R. Fitzpatrick.

V-80

TAKE ME TO CZECHOSLOVAKIA, DRIVER

YES SIR!

V-80, V-81 *Field Marshal Goering called Shoemaker's work "horrible examples" of anti-Nazi propaganda in the United States.*

was particularly effective when employing massive symbols; Shoemaker used a delicate brush and generally filled his drawings with realistic details. But both agreed that America's best interests would not be served by appeasing a dictator.

Once America entered the war, cartoons became predictably bland. "Ding" Darling won the 1943 Pulitzer Prize for an attack on excessive governmental paperwork, one of the rare issues on which there could hardly be dissent. The only really exceptional cartooning was done by Sgt. Bill Mauldin, whose "Willie and Joe" showed the people back home what war looked like from a foxhole.

Most exciting of the postwar cartoonists was Herbert L. Block, better known

as "Herblock." He had been cartooning for newspapers since 1929, had taken a strong anti-Hitler stand in the '30s, and had even won a Pulitzer Prize in 1942 while working for the Newspaper Enterprise Association, a syndicate service. But he did not reach his full stride until joining the Washington *Post* in 1946.

Besides pure talent, wide syndication, and the full backing of his home paper, Herblock was to show that he had the courage to spend his influence on an issue that many other cartoonists chose to give a wide berth. As the nation reacted to the shock of the Cold War, a junior U.S. senator from Wisconsin set off on an unprincipled, publicity-grabbing hunt for domestic Communists and "fellow-travelers," thus giving the country a bad case of the shakes and the lexicographers a new word—"McCarthyism." In this charged atmosphere, the call to reason was best exemplified by another word —"Herblock."

For sheer impact, a nation's capital is the ideal place for a political cartoonist, and as cartoonist on the only morning paper in Washington, Herblock had a special breakfast-table readership: President, Cabinet, Congress, Supreme Court, diplomatic corps, national reporters. In an October, 1958, press conference in Minneapolis, Vice President Richard M. Nixon commented on the hardships of public figures and their

V-81

PATH OF APPEASEMENT

families. He was not complaining for himself, he said, but it was "difficult when your 10-year-old daughter comes home from school and says her classmates are teasing her about a cartoon in the morning paper." Two years later, when he was the Republican nominee, Nixon is reported to have said in discussing his campaign strategy, "I have to erase the Herblock image." If this was the case, it was the first time since 1884 that a candidate ran for President against a cartoonist.[15]

Although many cartoonists might have been wrong on Hitler and timid on McCarthy, on one crucial issue they

"I Have Here In My Hand ——"

V-82

V-83

"Here He Comes Now"

"Put It ON Again!!!!"

V-84 *Starting in 1924 and for the next twenty-four years, Edmund Duffy's powerful cartoons (influenced by his teacher, Boardman Robinson) appeared in the Baltimore* Sun *and earned him three Pulitzer Prizes. Around Baltimore, Gerald W. Johnson recalled, the cartoonist "was regarded with the uneasy delight that a zoo keeper has in a particularly fine Bengal tiger. A municipal asset, unquestionably, but everyone shuddered to think what would happen if he ever went on a rampage."*

have consistently spoken with force and eloquence. Long before it was front-page news, the vast majority of them were passionate advocates of Civil Rights. In the 1920s and 1930s men like Clive Weed of *Judge,* Edmund Duffy of the Baltimore *Sun,* Jacob Burck, and Reginald Marsh directed some of the most devastating attacks in the annals of American cartooning at the Ku Klux Klan.

From the school desegregation cases of the 1950s through the sit-ins of the 1960s, the cartoonists proved that they were again capable of moral commitment. Particularly courageous were some of the cartoonists of the upper South and border states whose views could hardly have met with complete approval in their communities: Bill Sanders of the Greensboro, North Carolina, *Daily News* (now with the Milwaukee *Journal*); Clifford H. Baldowski (Baldy) of the Atlanta, Georgia, *Constitution*; Robert York, Louisville, Kentucky, *Times;* Tom Little, Nashville *Tennessean,* and others.

In the North, too, effective work was done by such cartoonists as Paul Conrad (Denver *Post,* Los Angeles *Times*), Guersey le Pelley (*Christian Science Monitor*), Thomas Flannery (Baltimore *Evening Sun*), and Pierre Bellocq (Peb) of the Philadelphia *Inquirer.* But for sheer impact, one man's name stood above his colleagues. Just as the 1950s had been the Herblock decade in Ameri-

V-85 *Reginald Marsh, called "the pictorial laureate of the sidewalks of New York," filled small etchings and large oils with the same sense of pulsation that he brought to his* New Yorker *cartoons. Even after being recognized as one of the nation's foremost artists, he dissected corpses at a medical school "in order to draw them better."*

can cartooning, when an artist's talents had meshed perfectly with a dominant issue, so in the 1960s, when *the* issue was Civil Rights, *the* cartoonist was Bill Mauldin, first of the St. Louis *Post-Dispatch*, then of the Chicago *Sun-Times*.

While Mauldin masterfully ridiculed the southern redneck—who administered a *literacy* test to keep Negroes off the voting books without knowing "what's that big word?"—a northern white liberal named Jules Feiffer was brilliantly probing the rhetoric and psychology of northern white liberals, finding contradictions that went to the very depths of the race issue.

With the decline in the number of daily newspapers published each year in the United States and the subsequent loss of jobs and competition; with the rise in syndication and the subsequent loss of local angle material and proving grounds for young talent; with the competition from other media and the relative loss of importance and prestige; with an editorial caution bred of a healthy respect for libel laws and the real or imagined pressures from readers, advertisers, and the "front office,"

V-86   "SEE YOU IN CHURCH."

V-87

"I'VE DECIDED I WANT MY SEAT BACK."

V-86 (TOP), V-87   *Bill Mauldin, the World War II wunderkind who won a Pulitzer Prize at twenty-three, had a hard time adjusting to civilian life. He tried his hand at movie acting and politicking (running for Congress as a Democrat in a heavily Republican New York district). Not until he replaced Fitzpatrick on the St. Louis* Post-Dispatch *in 1958 —winning a second Pulitzer Prize the next year—was it clear that, as German cartoonist Paul Flora said, "He may outlast us all."*

V-88 *A hero of Greenwich Village since 1956, when his work began appearing in the weekly* Village Voice, *Jules Feiffer started his career by drawing for comic books, an experience that had an obvious effect on his style, which is noted for a great deal of ballooonless dialogue.*

the American newspaper cartoon has heard itself declared mortally ill so many times that even some of its practitioners are apt to accept the diagnosis.

Viewed from the long historical perspective there is only one thing wrong with this analysis: It is not true.

There is always the temptation to compare today with *all* of yesterday—a single season's baseball players with the Hall of Fame roster, one Senate with all the statesmen who were ever elected to office. But there were never more than a handful of first-rate cartoonists at any one time in American history. Usually there were not even two superb cartoonists at a given moment in time. Nast was in decline when

Keppler was in ascendancy; both were no longer drawing when Opper and Davenport did their best work; Kirby was dominant in the 1920s, Fitzpatrick in the '30s.

Now let us look at today.

There are roughly a hundred full-time editorial cartoonists. As in every era, many of them are merely trying to get through life without ruffling any feathers. They illustrate the news rather than make any attempt to mold it. Many lack talent and moral commitment. On the other hand, today in the United States there are possibly twenty artists (certainly fifteen) who often have something to say and have the ability to say it. Out of this number

A NEW HOT LINE FROM THE WHITE HOUSE —— TO CAPITOL HILL

V-89   *John Fischetti, 1963.*

there are perhaps a dozen (certainly a half-dozen) who almost always have a good deal to say and possess considerable talent. Moreover, there are several artists who will rate with the nation's all-time greats, and there are several others who have the potential to enter this select circle.

Herblock and Mauldin, the most widely reproduced cartoonists, have already staked claims in the annals of their profession; Feiffer makes a unique contribution as a commentator on the urban middle class; and among the others who draw rather consistently with humor and polish are Ed Valtman of the Hartford *Times*, Ray Osrin, Cleveland *Plain Dealer*, Robert Bastian,

San Francisco *Chronicle*, Gib Crockett, Washington *Star*, Robert Zschiesche, Greensboro, North Carolina, *Daily News*, Bill Sanders, Milwaukee *Journal*, Frank Interlandi, Los Angeles *Times*, an artist of rare intensity, Tom Darcy, Philadelphia *Bulletin*, and John Fischetti, Chicago *Daily News*, whose work sometimes resembles Bernard Buffet's in its accented vertical strokes and bold outlining of figures.

Furthermore, there is more experimentation today than there has been in many years, perhaps since the pre-World War I days of *The Masses*: the high degree of abstraction in the cartoons of Isadore Parker, Washington *Post*; the attempts of Hugh Haynie,

"There's no room in the shelter!"

V-90   *Frank Interlandi, 1961.*

'We Will Fight to the Last Vietnamese Any U.S. Attempt for a Negotiated Peace!'

V-91   *Edmund S. Valtman, 1965.*

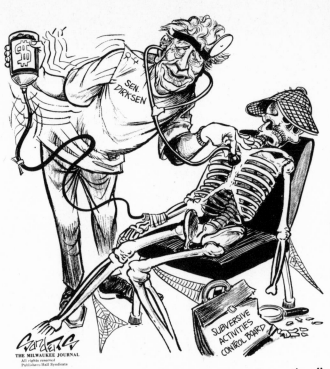

'*Courage lad. You'll be good as new in no time!*'

"BESIDES, THINK OF ALL THOSE COMMODITIES
FALLING OFF THE EDGE OF THE EARTH"

V-93   *Ray Osrin, 1967.*

'I'll guard the fort, Gene—you go down and see what they wan[t]

V-94   *Tom Darcy, 1968.*

Louisville *Courier-Journal*, and the editorial page staff of the Worcester, Massachusetts, *Telegram* and its cartoonist, Draper Hill, to deal differently with space; the proto-Victorian style of David Levine, most of whose caricatures appear in the *New York Review of Books;* and Jerry Robinson's political cartoons, "Still Life," in which only inanimate objects are seen.

The state of the art also holds special promise because so many of today's skillful professionals are in their twenties and thirties. Paul Szep, the Canadian with the Hungarian name who draws for the Boston *Globe*, is only twenty-seven; the Denver *Post's* Pat Oliphant won the Pulitzer Prize in 1967

WORCESTER TELEGRAM

Established May 19, 1886.
Published by the Worcester Telegram & Gazette, Inc.

H. G. STODDARD, Honorary Chairman
ROBERT W. STODDARD, Chairman   RICHARD C. STEELE, President and Publisher
FORREST W. SEYMOUR, Editor   GORDON A. O'BRIEN, Vice Pres., General Manager
ROBERT W. BOOTH, Vice President - Radio

Page 6   TUESDAY, MARCH 15, 1966

That Personal Touch

Charles de Gaulle broods much over history and his place in it. He may have won himself at least a footnote in the history books by his summary decision to write personal letters in longhand to President Johnson, Prime Minister Wilson, Chancellor Erhard, and President Saragat, informing them that all foreign bases must be removed from French soil.

The fact that he made this momentous move without telling his foreign ministry about it gives a touch of Louis XIV to the affair. Like many of De Gaulle's policies recently, this one fits in with the modern age about as aptly as a 17th Century wig.

The other western allies now must wait to see how far De Gaulle intends to push toward disintegration of the North Atlantic Treaty Organization. He may pull back at the brink, although it would be wise not to count on restraint. The old man is far gone in his dreams of French "grandeur" and his own omnipotence.

Nevertheless, the allies apparently are making discreet contingency plans to restructure NATO around the United States, Britain and West Germany. De Gaulle may not be able to conceive constructive policies, but he certainly can be destructive. He can pull French troops out of NATO and West Germany, and he can force NATO troops to leave French soil. If that happens, of course, France could no longer count on automatic NATO protection against attack.

Not the least of the consequences of the De Gaulle ploy will be the corresponding rise in importance of West Germany in western military and diplomatic councils. It is hard to see

why any French statesman would want this to happen, but as France pulls out, the vacuum seems almost certain to be filled by West German power.

Those handwritten letters may have consequences far beyond what the writer intended.

V-95   *Most mornings the basic shape of the Worcester* Telegram's *editorial page is designed around what is thought to be the best dimension for Draper Hill's cartoon. Should it be vertical or horizontal? Should it be a single column, or two, three, or four columns? Here the drawing is used as a "footnote" right in the editorial.*

Two cartoons of Charles de Gaulle illustrate new attempts to deal with old problems.

"If You Won't Play My Way I'll Take My Ball And Go Home"

V-96   *Hugh Haynie began newspaper cartooning in 1952 and, like many other young artists of that time, had to overcome a stylistic reliance on Herblock. The distinctive technique that emerged uses oddly placed "picture frames" to redefine or break out of the cartoon's normal boundaries. (Note that he weaves his wife's name—Lois—into his drawing; this technique is also used by Paul Szep, whose wife is Ann.)*

still life

what is a limited war?

that's one where the casualties don't exceed the birth rate

V-97 *Jerry Robinson's "Still Life," created in 1963, is political without being dependent on the morning's headline. During the so-called Golden Age of Comic Books, he helped draw Batman and invented that archvillain The Joker.*

V-98 *"Any time I can bring a god down to human scale, so people can say, 'Gee, Johnson has big ears, just like my kid,' I'm delighted," comments David Levine, the New York artist who has almost single-handedly revived the caricature form. His deceptively soft, deliberately whimsical technique generally focuses on literary figures. But he aims at enough politicians and employs just enough "props" (the Vietnam scar, for example) to qualify as a political cartoonist.*

CUPID

V-99   *Wayne Stayskal, 1967.*

V-100   *Paul Szep, 1967.*

*"A Senator Fulbright to see you, Sire.
Seems he can't reconcile himself to your
infallibility."*

at the age of thirty-one; Draper Hill is thirty-three; Tom Darcy is thirty-five; Bill Sanders is thirty-eight; and Wayne Stayskal of *Chicago's American*, who served his apprenticeship under Vaughn Shoemaker, is now thirty-seven.

Then, too, the cartooning profession now has two artists who appear destined to add new luster to the comic tradition in America. Paul Conrad, an Iowan who ingested "Ding" Darling's cartoons with his Pablum, started drawing in 1950 for the Denver *Post*, where it soon became evident that he combined a broad sense of humor with the ability to stay fighting mad most of the time. When he moved to the Los Angeles *Times* in 1964 he was replaced in Denver, after a six-month talent hunt, by the twenty-nine-year-old cartoonist for the Adelaide (Australia) *Advertiser*. Incredibly, two years later Patrick B. Oliphant, the transported Australian, won the highest cartooning honor in the United States, the Pulitzer Prize. (It was another case, however, of a brilliant cartoonist's winning with a mundane piece of work, proving again the Pulitzer committee's penchant for the inferior. The secret story behind the cartoon is that Oliphant and his wife studied a book of Pulitzer Prize winners and settled on a design that could be expected to please the judges, though hardly themselves. Oliphant then suppressed the natural drollery that is his trademark and produced a picture of Ho Chi Minh holding a dying Vietnamese in his arms, saying: "They won't get *us* to the conference table . . . will they?" As predicted, it was chosen the best editorial cartoon drawn in the United States during 1966.)

Over a century ago *The Nation* magazine concluded, "Humor is not usually a quality of virtuous indignation; and great immoralities, public or private, are not to be dealt with in a spirit of levity, because to subject them to the ordeal of ridicule, would be really to diminish the abhorrence with which they should be regarded."[16] Nearly eighty years have passed since Henry James wrote that there was no such thing as American caricature.[17] The illustrious journal and the distinguished novelist were mistaken. Americans not only have had the capacity to poke fun

V-101, V-102   In two cartoons, drawn six months apart, Paul Conrad chose the Iwo Jima flag raising and proved not only his versatility but his firm place in the long tradition of American punsters. The cartoon on the left is titled "Flag Razing in Central Park." The cartoon of "Ky's Cabinet," right, prompted a letter from Boise, Idaho: "Don't you know the lock on an outhouse is on the inside?" Conrad's publisher's wife also got an irate letter from a Los Angeles woman who was "shocked" that the soldier on the right had a "nude bottom." (She enclosed the offending cartoon, having encircled what she thought was the exposed portion of the anatomy.)

at their politics and their politicians, but they have often done it exceedingly well. Moreover, it has been therapeutic. Yet having proved that American political cartoons have had a past, what can one say of the future? Prediction is impossible. For the history of the ungentlemanly art is primarily the collective history of its artists. And, beyond comment on those who are drawing today, one can only reaffirm C. D. Batchelor's belief that "a political cartoonist should have in him a little of the clown, the poet, the historian, the artist, and the dreamer."[18] It is a rare amalgam, not one to which man has been given the formula. Or, as Frederick Richardson said about the cartoonist at the turn of the century, "It is lucky for him that he is born and not made, for the making would be a laborious process."[19]

V-103 *Pat Oliphant manages to draw a cartoon within a cartoon through his invention, Punk the Penguin, a character with his own views on the subject matter. Oliphant says this technique gives him "a chance to get in a secondary comment which is supplementary" to the caption.*

'I'LL TELL YOU THIS MUCH—YOU'D NEVER GET ME UP IN ONE OF THEM THINGS!'

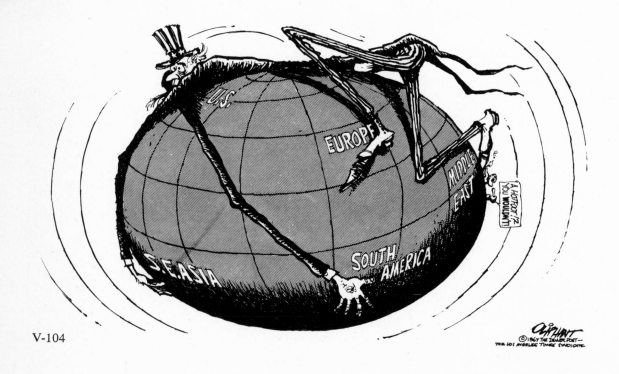

V-104

170

I

"Them Damn Pictures"

I-1   Thomas Nast (1840–1902),
"Who Stole the People's Money?"
wood engraving, Harper's Weekly,
Aug. 19, 1871.

I-1A   In an interesting instance of a
cartoon inspiring a cartoon, Edwin
Marcus (1885–1961) goes back to
Nast's "Who Stole the People's
Money?" in order to compare the
leaders of Germany during World
War I with Tweed Ring. The New
York Times, Dec. 15, 1918.

"Who caused the war?—'Twas him"

I-2   Thomas Nast, "Tweed-le-dee
and Tilden-dum," wood engraving,
Harper's Weekly, July 1, 1876.

1. Nast never fully credited the
account of Tweed's capture until
years later when he received
confirmation in a letter dated Jan.
28, 1892, from Alvey A. Adee, who
had been Secretary of the American
Legation at Madrid. See Albert
Bigelow Paine, "Th. Nast: His
Period and His Pictures (New York
& London: Harper, 1904), p. 337;
also see Alexander B. Callow, Jr.,
The Tweed Ring (New York:
Oxford University Press, 1966), and
J. Chal Vinson, Thomas Nast,
Political Cartoonist (Athens:
University of Georgia Press, 1967).

2. Isabel Simeral Johnson,
"Caricature and Cartoon," in
Contemporary Cartoons: An
Exhibition of Original Drawings of
American Artists at the Huntington
Library (San Marino, California:
Henry E. Huntington Library and
Art Gallery, 1937), p. 34.

3. For the works of Hogarth, see
Ronald Paulson, Hogarth's Graphic
Works (New Haven: Yale University
Press, 1965), 2 vols.; The World of
Hogarth, Lichtenberg's
Commentaries on Hogarth's
Engravings (Boston: Houghton
Mifflin, 1967); and Frederick Antal,
Hogarth and His Place in European
Art (London: Routledge & Kegan
Paul, 1962).

I-3   William Hogarth (1697–1764),
"Canvassing for Votes," from the
Election Series, 1757. Engraving by
C. Grignion, The Works of William
Hogarth from the Original Plates
(London: Bledwin & Cradock,
n.d.)

4. For the works of Gillray, see
Draper Hill, Mr. Gillray, The
Caricaturist (London: Phaidon,

1965), and his *Fashionable Contrasts, Caricatures by James Gillray* (London: Phaidon, 1966).

I-4   *James Gillray (1756–1815),* "*Black-Dick Turn'd Taylor*" *(detail), engraving, 1788, in* The Works of James Gillray from the Original Plates (*London: Henry G. Bohn, 1851*), *plate 26.*

I-5   *John Leech (1817–64),* "*Cartoon No. 1. Substance and Shadow,*" *wood engraving,* Punch, or the London Charivari, *July 15, 1843.*

5. Even today a number of the best cartoonists working in the U.S. press are foreign-born, such as Patrick Oliphant of the Denver *Post* (an Australian), Edmund Valtman, Hartford *Times* (Estonian), and Paul Szep, Boston *Globe* (Canadian). On the other hand, only one American has built a major reputation abroad: Livingston Hopkins (1846–1927), who was the cartoonist for the Sydney (Australia) *Bulletin* from 1882 until his death. According to another cartoonist, Hopkins became a millionaire. See Walt McDougall, *This Is the Life!* (New York: Knopf, 1926), pp. 72–3.

6. The authors wish to acknowledge Herbert A. Kenny of the Boston *Globe* for information on Norman Ritchie. For information on Tom Vidro, we are grateful to Gerald A. Elliott of the Grand Rapids *Press*.

7. Hugh S. Fullerton, "Answering the Query: Are Cartoonists Human?" *Collier's,* Nov. 8, 1924, p. 8.

8. See John Chase, "Jim Berryman" in *Today's Cartoon* (New Orleans: Hauser Press, 1962), pages unnumbered. Clifford Berryman's daughter Florence was also connected with the Washington *Evening Star,* as an art critic, for many years. See *Newsweek,* Aug. 9, 1943, p. 74.

I-6   *Fay King, self-portrait,* Cartoons Magazine, *Mar., 1918.*

9. John Ames Mitchell, "Contemporary American Caricature," *Scribner's Magazine,* Dec., 1889, p. 734.

10. See *Puck,* Aug. 25, 1886, pp. 8–9. C. D. Batchelor, the Pulitzer Prize-winning cartoonist for the New York *Daily News,* once built an entire cartoon around the drawing of a hand, which, on close inspection, is seen to have six fingers. New Britain (Conn.) *Herald,* Nov. 5, 1955.

11. Frank Beard, "Caricature," *The Manhattan,* Feb., 1884, p. 140.

I-7   *George Luks (1867–1933),* "*Hanna: That man Clay was an ass. It's better to be President than to be right!*" The Verdict, *Mar. 13, 1899.*

I-8   *John Sloan (1871–1951), cover,* The Masses, *June, 1914.*

12. See Coulton Waugh, *The Comics* (New York: Macmillan, 1947), p. 23. George Luks also was a comic-strip artist for a few years, having been hired by Joseph Pulitzer's New York *World* to draw *The Yellow Kid* in the 1890s.

13. Rollin Kirby, "My Creed as a Cartoonist," *Pep,* Dec., 1918, p. 16, and "J. N. Darling on Editorial Ideas" in Gene Byrnes, *The Complete Guide to Cartooning* (New York: Grosset & Dunlap, 1950), p. 78. On the other hand, for those who have argued for the preeminence of draftsmanship in cartooning, see Boardman Robinson, "America's Foremost Cartoonist Talks on Our Cartooning Art, and Tells Why It Misses Being Great," *Pep,* Nov., 1917, pp. 3, 5, and Jacob Burck, "Cartooning Is Like This," *The Masthead,* Winter 1950, p. 36.

I-9   *Bill Mauldin (b. 1921),* "*Fresh, spirited American troops, flushed with victory, are bringing in thousands of hungry, ragged, battle-weary prisoners. . . . (News item),*" *United Features Syndicate, Nov. 8, 1944. See* The *New York Times, June 27, 1945, p. 21.*

I-10   *Samuel L. Clemens (Mark Twain) (1835–1910),* "*William III, King of Prussia,*" Galaxy, *Jan., 1871. Widener Library, Harvard University.*

I-11   *William Sydney Porter (O. Henry) (1862–1910),* "*Can He Make the Jump?*" The Rolling Stone, *Oct. 13, 1894. University of Texas, Austin. See A. de Ford Pitney,* "*O. Henry as a Cartoonist,*" Cartoons Magazine, *Apr., 1917, pp. 509–15, and Frank Luther Mott,* A History of American Magazines, *Volume IV: 1885–1905 (Cambridge: Harvard University Press, 1957), pp. 665–70.*

I-12   *Enrico Caruso (1873–1921),* "*Roosevelt,*" Caricatures by Enrico Caruso (*New York: La Fallia di New York, 1908*).

14. See J. M. Baer, "Cartoons and Success," *Pep,* Aug., 1919, p. 2; and *Cartoons Magazine,* Sept., 1917, p. 428.

I-13   *John M. Baer (b. 1886),* "*Learned Senators—This Picture Is for You,*" Washington Times, *Jan. 7, 1918. The caption reads: "Take good care of the spigot, watch that tiny drop by all means. BUT, don't forget the bunghole on the side. See if you can't do something there. You are considering this week the proposition that the nation's property should be given away for private exploitation —oil, coal, potassium and other products worth hundreds and perhaps thousands of millions of dollars. Forget the spigot for a minute, move around to the bunghole and see if you can't stop that loss and waste of national wealth. If YOU don't stop it, other Senators will be sent here that will stop it. The people are in no mood for trifling."*

15. *Congressional Record,* Oct. 3, 1913, p. 5382, and "The Cartoon That Got into the Congressional Record," *Cartoons Magazine,* Dec., 1913, pp. 666–67.

I-13A *Senator Tillman's cartoon (shown here as it appeared in Congressional Record) was actually drawn by Tom Fleming and first appeared in the New York World, Mar. 1, 1896.*

SENATOR TILLMAN'S ALLEGORICAL COW.

16. Jules Feiffer, "Our Age of Violence," *The New York Times,* Apr. 23, 1967, Sec. II, p. 1.

17. Among the other political cartoonists who switched to the comics have been Paul Fung (*Polly and Her Pals*), Vernon Greene (*Bringing Up Father*), Johnny Gurelle (*Brutus*), Harry Haenigsen (*Penny, Our Bill*), T. E. Powers (*Let the Wedding Bells Ring Out*), Harry Tuthill (*The Bungle Family*), and Charles H. Winner (*Elmer*).

18. See Milton A. McRae, *Forty Years in Newspaperdom* (New York: Brentano's, 1924), p. 43.

19. Cecil Jensen's comic strip was *Little Debbie;* Tom Little drew *Sunflower Street.* See Mel Heimer, *Famous Artists and Writers of King Features Syndicate* (New York: King Features, 1946). For biographical information on Reuben L. (Rube) Goldberg (b. 1883), see "Answer to the Question: How Did You Put It Over?" *American Magazine,* Mar., 1922, and "It Happened to a Rube," *Saturday Evening Post,* Nov. 10, 1929; also *Newsweek,* Dec. 5, 1938, p. 27, and *Editor & Publisher,* Sept. 21, 1940, p. 40. Franklin O. Alexander, the Philadelphia *Bulletin's* political cartoonist from 1941 until 1967, first drew *Hairbreadth Harry* for eight years, but he was not that comic strip's creator.

20. Rollin Kirby in *Catalogue of the Salon of American Humorists* (New York: The College Art Association, 1933), p. 62.

I-14 *Richard F. Outcault (1863–1928), "The War Scare in Hogan's Alley," New York World, Mar. 15, 1896. See Harry J. Westerman, "Outlines Career of R. F. Outcalt [sic], Ohio-born Artist," The Ohio Newspaper, Dec., 1933.*

21. Richard L. Neuberger, "Hooverism in the Funnies," *The New Republic*, July 11, 1934, pp. 234–35.

I-15 *Harold Gray (1894–1968), Orphan Annie, Chicago Tribune– New York News Syndicate, June 13, 1967.*

I-16 *Al Capp (b. 1909), Li'l Abner, Chicago Tribune–New York News Syndicate, Nov. 13, 1965. See David Manning White,* From Dogpatch to Slobbovia, The World of Li'l Abner *(Boston: Beacon, 1964); Frank Brady, "How Li'l Abner Got His Start,"* The Quill, *Oct., 1937, p. 12; Robert L. Levey, "The Man From D.O.G.P.A.T.C.H.,"* Boston Sunday Globe Magazine, *Nov. 19, 1967, pp. 18–19.*

I-17 *Chester Gould (b. 1900), Dick Tracy, Chicago Tribune– New York News Syndicate, June 29, 1967. For biographical information on Chester Gould and Harold Gray, see Martin Sheridan,* Comics and Their Creators *(Hale, Cushman & Flint, 1942), pp. 121–22, 69–70.*

22. Walt Kelly, *The Ever-Lovin' Blue-Eyed Years with Pogo* (New York: Simon & Schuster, 1959), p. 135. For an example of Kelly's Thomas Dewey as the mechanical man, see New York *Star*, July 26, 1948.

I-18 *Walter Crawford Kelly, Jr. (b. 1913), Pogo, Publishers-Hall Syndicate, May 7, 1953.*

23. Arthur Bartlett Maurice and Frederick Taber Cooper, *The History of the Nineteenth Century in Caricature* (New York: Dodd, Mead, 1904), p. 4.

24. See William Murrell, *A History of American Graphic Humor* (New York: Whitney Museum of Art,

1933), I, pp. 52–3.

I-19 *Civil War Envelopes, wood engraving: 1, "Good 'Noose' for Traitors"; 2, "Music by the 'Contra-Band' "; 3, "Deaf Man—I have got the Secession Fever . . ."*

25. See *Editor & Publisher*, Dec. 16, 1939, p. 10.

I-20 *Max Bachmann (d. 1921), "United for the National Honor,"* Leslie's Weekly Illustrated, *Oct. 1, 1896. For another example of his clay cartoons, see* Harper's Weekly, *Aug. 22, 1908.*

I-21 *"Would you buy a used guitar from this man?"* Republican Congressional Committee Newsletter, *July 17, 1967. United Press International photograph by Stanley Stearns, July 11, 1967.*

I-22 *Gerald Gardner, "In 1492,"* Who's in Charge Here? *(New York: Pocket Books, 1962).*

I-22A *A page from a cartoon book that supporters of Republican Governor John Chafee put out in 1964 to show voters in traditionally Democratic Rhode Island how to split their tickets. (below)* Let's Re-elect Governor Chafee Handbook, *drawing by Dan Wulf, based on an idea by Mrs. Peter Gutlon. The authors thank James Marshall, former press secretary to Governor Chafee, for this information. In the same year the Democratic Party in traditionally Republican Maine printed a cartoon book entitled,* The Maine Thing, Some of Our Best Friends Are Republicans.

ALL THE PEOPLE LIKED HIM BECAUSE HE WAS FAIR AND TOOK CARE OF EVERYONE, NOT JUST ONE PART OF THE PEOPLE, OR JUST ONE PARTY.

26. See William L. Bloomer, *A Souvenir Containing Cartoons Issued by the Press Bureau of the Ohio State Republican Executive Committee* (Columbus, Ohio, 1899). Bloomer was a well-known Buckeye cartoonist who, besides working for the State G.O.P., was employed at various times by the Ohio State *Journal* (Columbus), the Cleveland *Press,* and the Scripps-McRae Syndicate, covering the Spanish-American War in Cuba and Puerto Rico.

27. *The New York Times,* May 3, 1950, p. 25. Cartoonists have made notoriously bad political party employees. W. Gordon Nye, hired by the Democratic National Committee during the 1904 Presidential campaign, later supported the Republican. See B. O. Flower, "W. Gordon Nye: A Cartoonist of Jeffersonian Democracy," *The Arena,* Aug., 1906.

28. While the TV picture flashed from one editorial cartoon of Rockefeller to another, the Governor's voice was heard saying, "For the past eight years, New York State has been governed by this strange-looking gentleman. This is me, as you may have seen me in the papers. You notice I have my ups and downs. When I open a new road, when I announce new state scholarships or a pure waters program, somehow a twinkle comes into my eye. Why, there seems to be something *likeable* about me. But when I veto someone's pet project, or knock an item out of the budget or sign a bill to get the money to pay for the scholarships, my portrait gets painted a little differently. The plain fact of the matter is, if you want to be a good governor, you're gonna [sic] make some people mad." This was prepared by the New York

advertising agency of Jack Tinker & Partners. See Myron McDonald, "The Magic of Hard-Hitting Political Television Spots," in *The Art of Winning Elections* (Washington: Republican National Committe, 1967), pp. 84–5.

29. Scott Long, "The Cartoon Is a Weapon," *The Masthead,* Fall, 1961, p. 16.

30. Don Hesse, "The Ungentlemanly Art," *The Quill,* Dec., 1959, p. 7.

I-23   *Page two of* The Coon Dissector, *Dayton, Ohio, wood engravings, Aug. 23, 1844.*

I-23A   *Henry Clay's Whigs in Dayton countered* The Coon Dissector *with a newspaper in praise of the coon's virtues.*

I-24 Herbert L. Block (Herblock) (b. 1909), "Don't Mind Me—Just Go Right on Talking," Washington Post, Feb. 5, 1947.

I-25 Herbert L. Block, "It Looks Darling," Washington Post, Sept. 3, 1954. See Herbert Block, The Herblock Book (Boston: Beacon, 1952), p. 34.

31. Albert Mathews, Brother Jonathan (Cambridge, Mass.: John Wilson & Son, 1902), p. 28; see also his Uncle Sam (Worcester, Mass.: Davis Press, 1908).

I-26 Amos Doolittle (1754–1832), "Brother Jonathan Administering a Salutary Cordial To John Bull," 1813, engraving. American Antiquarian Society, Worcester, Mass. For information about the artist, see William A. Beardsley, An Old New Haven Engraver and His Work: Amos Doolittle (photostatic copy, Library of Congress, Dec. 19, 1910), and J. V. Whitaker, "American Caricatures, II," Leisure Hour, Oct. 21, 1876, p. 687.

I-27 "Uncle Sam in Danger," 1834, lithograph. American Antiquarian Society, Worcester, Mass. See William Murrell, "Rise and Fall of Cartoon Symbols," The American Scholar, Summer, 1935, pp. 310–11. The cartoon in which Uncle Sam and Brother Jonathan appear together is "Uncle Sam Sick with La Grippe," published by H. R. Robinson, circa 1836.

I-28 "Uncle Sam's Pet Pups, Or, Mother Bank's last refuge," 1840, woodcut.

I-29 John Tenniel (1820–1914), "Lincoln's Two Difficulties," wood engraving, Punch, or The London Charivari, Aug. 23, 1862.

I-30 Charles Dana Gibson (1867–1944), "His mother: 'Here he is, Sir,' " Life, Apr. 19, 1917. The model for the young man was the artist's son, Langhorne Gibson, who, following the cartoon's advice, left Yale to enlist in the Navy. This cartoon was made into a 28-inch-by-41-inch Navy recruiting poster, captioned, "Here he is, Sir. We need him and you too." Gibson began his career as a political cartoonist for Tid-Bits, a staunchly Republican humor magazine of the middle 1880's, but he had little interest in politics and his work was not exceptional. The one thing he liked about political cartooning, according to his biographer, was that it gave him an opportunity to draw animals, especially the Republican elephant. Although Gibson gave up political cartooning to do his famous "Gibson girls," he did draw some effective anti-German cartoons for Life during World War I. See Thomas Craven, Cartoon Cavalcade (New York: Simon & Schuster, 1943), p. 14; Frank Weitenkampf, Manhattan Kaleidoscope (New York: Scribner's, 1947), pp. 160–61; and Fairfax Downey, Portrait of an Era as Drawn by C. D. Gibson (New York: Scribner's, 1936).

I-31 James Montgomery Flagg (1877–1960), "I Want You for U.S. Army," United States Army Recruiting Service, 1917, adapted from a cover for Leslie's Illustrated Weekly Newspaper, July 6, 1916. The model for Uncle Sam was the artist, who wrote that 4 million copies of the poster were printed in World War I and 350,000 in World War II. See his autobiography, Roses and Buckshot (New York: Putnam's, 1946), pp. 157–58.

32. Allan Nevins, "Let's Disown Uncle Sam," The New York Times Magazine, Mar. 1, 1959, pp. 12, 68; Rollin Kirby, "A Cartoonist Criticizes Our Cartoonists," Current Opinion, Apr., 1920, p. 532. For other articles on Uncle Sam, see Mary Swing Ricker, "Uncle Sam's in Cartoon," The World Today, Oct., 1910, and Mrs. D. Harry Hammer, "Cartoons of Uncle Sam," Cartoons Magazine, June, 1913.

I-32 John Childs, publisher, "Notice to Quit," lithograph, 1840. See The Log Cabin (New York), May 30, 1840.

I-32A In a somewhat earlier example of Jack Downing this symbol of the American people cheers President Jackson's removal of government deposits from the U.S. Bank. Lithograph published by H. R. Robinson, 1833.

THE DOWNFALL OF MOTHER BANK.

I-33 *Frederick Opper (1857–1937), "The Common People" in* Cartoons by Lovey *(Salt Lake City: Lovey Fund, 1907). See B. O. Flower, "Frederick Opper: A Cartoonist of Democracy,"* The Arena, *June, 1905, p. 502.*

I-34 *Will B. Johnstone (1881–1944), "We, the people speak!"* New York *World-Telegram, June 29, 1940. See "He Didn't Aim to Be a Cartoonist,"* The Quill, *July, 1940, pp. 8–9, 13. Wrote* The New York Times, *Feb. 8, 1944, of Johnstone's "taxpayer-in-the-barrell": "His plucked and pathetic little taxpayer seemed somehow to symbolize us all." A somewhat similar Joe Doakes appeared in the cartoons of the Philadelphia Bulletin's F. O. Alexander.*

I-35 *"The Modern Balaam and His Ass," 1837. It should be noted that although Nast did not invent the Democratic Donkey, he was its primary popularizer.*

I-35A *The donkey was first used by Nast to represent not specifically the Democratic party but the Copperheads (i.e., Democratic sympathizers with the South). Harper's Weekly, Jan. 15, 1870, wood engraving.*

"A LIVE JACKASS KICKING A DEAD LION."

I-36 *Thomas Nast, "The Third-Term Panic," wood engraving,* Harper's Weekly, *Nov. 7, 1874. In 1966 a Republican Congressional Committee press release stated, "Ever since Thomas Nast . . . came up with an elephant . . . to depict the Republican Party, the pachyderm has been the proud symbol of the Grand Old Party. But the GOP elephant never had a name." To rectify this oversight, the Committee held a contest (won by a lady from Oceanside, Cal.), and Nast's elephant was christened "Republic Ann."*

33. The History of the Republican Party (Washington: Republican National Committee, 1967), p. 52.

I-37 *Jim Berry (b. 1935), "Gettin' Back at the Cartoonists," pen and ink drawing,* Newspaper Enterprise Association, *1964.*

I-38. *Frederick Richardson (1862–1937), "The Property Room of the Clever Cartoonist,"* Chicago Daily News, *Jan. 14, 1899, reprinted in Frederick Richardson,* Book of Drawings *(Chicago: Lakeside Press, 1899).*

I-39 *"The sixteenth street distillery cow stables, cows and milkmaids, undergoing the process of whitewashing by Aldermen Tuomey, Tucker and Reed,"* Frank Leslie's Illustrated Newspaper, *July 17, 1858.*

I-40 *John T. McCutcheon (1870–1949), "Campaigning with Bathhouse John,"* Chicago Record-Herald, *Mar. 20, 1902, reprinted in* Cartoons by McCutcheon *(Chicago: McClurg, 1903). See Carter H. Harrison,* Stormy Years *(New York & Indianapolis: Bobbs-Merrill, 1935), pp. 158, 229.*

I-41 *Pete, "We are pure and high minded patriots persecuted by our political enemies!"* Wasp, *Dec. 1, 1906.*

I-42 *Clifford K. Berryman (1869–1949), "After One Hundred Fifty-Nine Years,"* Washington Star, *Apr. 19, 1934.*

I-42A *Berryman's inspiration was this F.O.C. Darley painting, "First Blow for Liberty," which had been widely circulated in the mid-nineteenth century through an engraving by A. H. Ritchie.*

I-43 Daniel R. Fitzpatrick (b. 1891), "Competition Hits East St. Louis's Rat Alley," St. Louis Post-Dispatch, Sept. 13, 1946.

I-44 Jacob Burck (b. 1904), "Hood Row. 'Let's not rub nobody out dis week, Boss, it's Brudderhood Week,'" Chicago Sun-Times, Feb. 18, 1952.

34. Ogden Nash in What! More Dahl (Boston: Robert T. Hale & Co., 1944). This, however, would not be the last time the poet found inspiration in a cartoonist: see "Jules Feiffer, I Love You" in Judith Viorst, The Village Square (New York: Coward-McCann, 1966). In another instance, cartoonist Art Young wrote "An Ode to Himself by Himself," The Masses, Dec., 1915, p. 21.

35. Walt Kelly, "Pogo Looks at the Abominable Snowman," in David Manning White and Robert A. Abel, eds., The Funnies (Glencoe, Ill.: The Free Press, 1963), p. 290.

36. See Albert B. Paine, Th. Nast: His Period and His Pictures, p. 129; James L. Ford, Forty-Odd Years in the Literary Shop (New York: Dutton, 1921), p. 209; and W. J. Arkell, Old Friends and Some Acquaintances (Los Angeles: privately printed, 1927), p. 59.

37. See Oswald G. Villard, Some Newspapers and Newspapermen (New York: Knopf, 1923), p. 51.

I-45 Ike Morgan (1871–1913), "Messrs. Klaw and Erlanger present 'Mr. Bluebeard,' Late of the Iroquois Theatre," Life, Jan. 21, 1904.

38. See Laws of Pennsylvania, Session of 1903, p. 353.

I-46 Charles Nelan (1854–1904), "It may well be doubted whether ever before in the history of American politics such an event (as my nomination) has occurred." Philadelphia North American, Oct. 19, 1902. Although Nelan, a native of Akron, achieved his greatest fame by drawing a Pennsylvania governor as a parrot, he first came into prominence by drawing an Ohio governor (Joseph Foraker) as a vulture. At the time Nelan was employed by the Cleveland Press. His best work was done for the New York Herald during the Spanish-American War and was compiled in book form, Cartoons of Our War with Spain (New York: Stokes, 1898). Also see Grant Wright, The Art of Caricature (New York: Baker Taylor, 1904), pp. 155–58.

I-46A It was revealed after Nelan's death that he had great difficulty drawing the female form and that all the women in his cartoons were done by his wife. New York Herald, Oct. 20, 1898.

PROTECTION WANTED—FROM WESTERN KISSERS.

I-47 *Walt McDougall
(1858–1938), "McDougall Shows
Pusey the Fatal Weakness of his
Anti-Cartoon Bill and Hurls
Defiance at Him," Philadelphia*
North American, *Jan. 30, 1903.*

39. See *Statutes of California, 1899,*
Chap. XXIX, and Frank Luther
Mott, *American Journalism* (New
York: Macmillan, 1950), p. 588.

I-48 *Homer Davenport
(1887–1912), "They Never Liked
Cartoons," New York* Journal and
Advertiser, *Apr. 22, 1897.*

I-49 *Homer Davenport, "There
Are Some Who Laugh and Others
Who Weep," New York* Journal and
Advertiser, *Apr. 25, 1897. Pen and
ink drawing.*

I-49A *Frank Spangler
(1881–1946), "Cartoon Mirror,"
Montgomery (Ala.) Advertiser,
Feb. 3, 1915. Department of
Archives and History, State of
Alabama, Montgomery. When
Spangler drew this cartoon, he wrote
that he would be looking for a new
job if the Alabama legislature
passed the proposed anti-cartoon
bill. But the bill did not pass and
Spangler remained one of the South's
leading cartoonists until his death
thirty-one years later.*

II

Copper Engraving and Woodcut 1747-1828

II-1 *Benjamin Franklin*
(*1706–90*), "Non Votis," *metal cut*,
Plain Truth, *1747.*

II-1A *This is how Franklin looked
at the time he drew the first
American political cartoon. Portrait
by Robert Feke (1724–69),
c. 1748, reproduced by permission
of the Fogg Museum of Art,
Harvard University.*

1. *The Autobiography of Benjamin Franklin* (New York: Garden City Pub. Co., 1939), pp. 130–32.

II-2   *Attributed to James Dove (1696–1769), "The Counter-Medly," 1764 (detail), engraving, Historical Society of Pennsylvania, Philadelphia.*

2. See Frank Luther Mott, *American Journalism, op. cit.,* p. 54. See also Albert Matthews, "The Snake Devices," Colonial Society of Massachusetts, *Publications, XI* (1906).

II-3   *Benjamin Franklin, "Join or Die," metal cut,* Pennsylvania Gazette, *May 9, 1754.*

II-4   *Masthead,* The Constitutional Courant, *Sept. 21, 1765, metal cut.*

II-5   *Paul Revere (1735–1818), masthead,* The Massachusetts Spy, *or Thomas's Boston Journal, July 7, 1774, metal cut.*

3. See William Murrell, "Rise and Fall of Cartoon Symbols," *op cit.,* p. 307.

II-5A   *James Gillray, "The American Rattle Snake," engraving, 1782, published by W. Humphrey, London.*

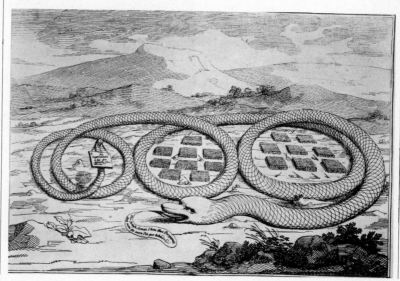

4. Another rider "on the eighteenth of April, in Seventy-five" was William Dawes, about whom a poet less famous than Longfellow wrote:

> 'Tis all very well for the children to hear
> Of the midnight ride of Paul Revere;
> But why should my name be quite forgot,
> Who rode as bold and well, God wot?
> Why should I ask? The reason is clear—
> My name was Dawes and his Revere.

See Clarence S. Brigham, *Paul Revere's Engravings* (Worcester, Mass.: American Antiquarian Society, 1954), pp. 3–4.

5. See Arthur M. Schlesinger, Sr., *Prelude to Independence, The Newspaper War on Britain, 1764–1776* (New York: Knopf, 1958), p. 43.

II-6 *Paul Revere, "The Bloody Massacre," engraving, 1770.*

II-6A *Revere's friend John Singleton Copley (1738–1815) probably did this portrait to pay off a debt he owed the silversmith, whom he painted in his work clothes—a rare pose in a day when people usually dressed in their finest when sitting for an artist. Probably painted around 1765. Courtesy Museum of Fine Arts, Boston. Gift of the Revere family. See Esther Forbes,* Paul Revere and the World He Lived In *(Boston: Houghton Mifflin, 1942), pp. 112–14.*

II-7 *"A Warm Place—Hell,"* engraving in The Scots Scourage, being a Compleat supplement to the British Antidote to Caledonian Poison, *London, 1765. American Antiquarian Society, Worcester, Mass.*

II-8 *Paul Revere, "A Warm Place-Hell," 1768, engraving, American Antiquarian Society, Worcester, Mass.*

II-9 *Paul Revere, untitled engraving,* Boston Gazette and Country Journal, *Mar. 12, 1770.*

6. William Bradford (1722–91) was the grandson of the founder of the first newspaper in New York and the son of the founder of the first newspaper in Philadelphia. He was to be known as the "patriot printer of 1776" because, at the age of fifty-six, he enlisted in the Revolutionary Army and was severely wounded at the battle of Princeton. See Stephen Hess, *America's Political Dynasties* (Garden City, N.Y.: Doubleday, 1966), p. 603.

II-10 Pennsylvania Journal, *Oct. 31, 1765, p. 1. The Historical Society of Pennsylvania, Philadelphia.*

II-10A *This grim theme was dusted off by enemies of Andrew Jackson during the 1828 Presidential race. The general-candidate's order to execute six deserters in the War of 1812 inspired this handbill.*

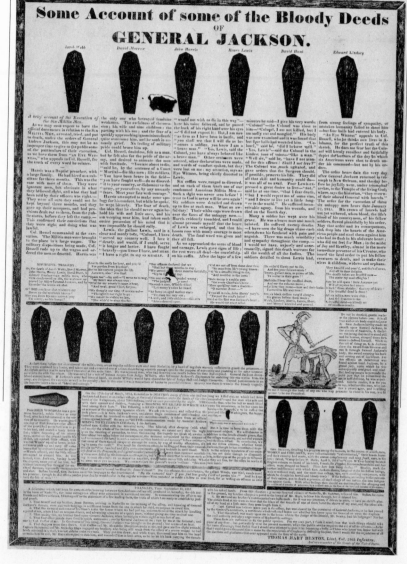

II-11 *W. Humphrey, publisher,*
"The Wise Men of Gotham and
Their Goose," London, 1776,
mezzotint. See Carl W. Drepperd,
Early American Prints (*New York*
& London: Century, 1930), pp.
206–08; The New York Times,
Feb. 26, 1933, II, p. 2; and R. T. H.
Halsey, "English Sympathy with
Boston During the American
Revolution," Old-Time New
England, *Apr.–June, 1956. Dutch*
artists also drew some pro-American
cartoons during the Revolutionary
War. See J. V. Whitaker, "American
Caricatures, I," Leisure Hour, *Sept.*
30, 1876, p. 636

7. Frank Weitenkampf, *Political*
Caricature in the United States
(New York: New York Public
Library, 1953). Also see his
"American Cartoons of To-day,"
Century, Feb., 1913, p. 542, and
Henry Ladd Smith, "The Rise and
Fall of the Political Cartoon,"
Saturday Review, May 29, 1954,
pp. 7–8.

8. The wood-cut process was
especially tedious, requiring
cartoons to be made in reverse and
fitted to exact measurements rather
than drawn to scale.

II-11A *In "Jonathan's Engraver,"*
readers of Yankee Notions (*Sept.,*
1852) were given this opportunity to
see how the magazine's wood cuts
were made.

9. Quoted in James Parton, *Caricature and Other Comic Art in All Times and Many Lands* (New York: Harper, 1878), p. 309.

10. See Allan Nevins and Frank Weitenkampf, *A Century of Political Cartoons* (New York: Scribner, 1944), pp. 20–1.

11. See James Melvin Lee, "Wordless Journalism, II," *Cartoons Magazine*, May, 1915, p. 736.

II-12   *Elkanah Tisdale (b. 1771). "The Gerry-mander," metal cut, Boston* Gazette, *Mar. 26, 1812.*

12. James Reichley, *States in Crisis* (Chapel Hill: University of North Carolina, 1964), p. 54.

13. William Murrell, *A History of American Graphic Humor, op. cit.,* I, 80.

II-13   *James Gillray, "Tiddy-doll the Great French Gingerbread-Baker, Drawing Out a New Batch of Kings," 1806, engraving. See Bohn, op. cit., plate 309.*

II-14   *William Charles (1776–1820), "John Bull Making a New Batch of Ships to Send to the Lakes," 1814, etching. For biographical information on Charles, see Harry B. Weiss,* William Charles, Early Caricaturist, Engraver and Publisher of Children's Books *(New York: New York Public Library, 1932). Also see William Murrell, "Foreword" to* Catalogue of the Salon of American Humorists, A Political and Social Pageant from the Revolution to the Present Day *(New York: The College Art Association, 1933), p. 17.*

II-15   *Thomas Rowlandson (1756–1827), "Marshalsea Prison," 1820 (detail), watercolor painting. Albert H. Wiggin Collection, Boston Public Library. See Arthur W.*

Heintzelman, The Watercolor Drawings of Thomas Rowlandson *(New York: Watson-Guptill, 1947).*

II-16   *William Charles, "Soldiers on a March to Buffalo," 1813 (detail), etching. Courtesy of the New-York Historical Society, New York City.*

II-17   *William Charles, "Queen Charlotte and Johnny Bull Get Their Dose of Perry," 1813, etching. Courtesy of the Historical Society of Pennsylvania, Philadelphia. See Frank Weitenkampf,* American Graphic Art *(New York: Holt, 1912), pp. 248–50.*

14. Clifford K. Berryman, "Development of the Cartoon," *University of Missouri Bulletin,* XXVII, No. 22 (June 7, 1926), p. 5.

II-18   *Elkanah Tisdale, "Infant Liberty Nursed by Mother Mob," engraving in John R. D. Huggins,* Hugginiana, *1808.*

II-18A   *Paul Revere's "The able Doctor, or America Swallowing the Bitter Draught,"* Royal American Magazine, *June, 1774, was based on this engraving in* London Magazine, *Apr., 1774 (detail).*

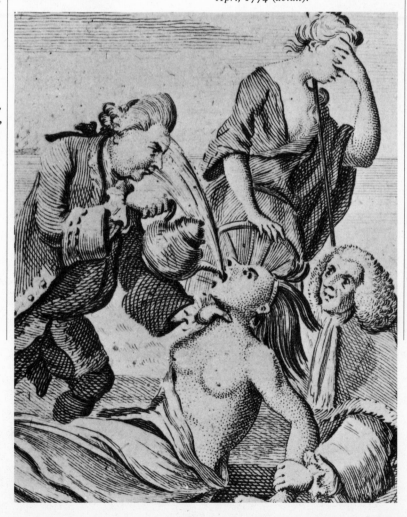

II-19 *John Childs, publisher, "Social Qualities of Our Candidate," 1852, lithograph.*

II-20 *Frank Bellew (1828–88), "Daniel in the Lion's Den," wood engraving,* The Lantern, *Aug. 14, 1852.*

II-21 *Matt Morgan (1828–90), "Our Modern Belshazzar," wood engraving,* Frank Leslie's Illustrated Newspaper, *Apr. 6, 1872 (detail).*

II-22 *Anthony Imbert, publisher, "The Doctor Puzzled or the Desperate Case of Mother U.S. Bank," 1833, lithograph.*

15. "The Limits of Caricature," *The Nation,* July 19, 1866, p. 55.

II-23 *"Born to Command. King Andrew the First," 1832, lithograph.*

II-24 *William Charles, "Josiah the First," 1812, etching. Josiah Quincy (1772–1864), Federalist congressman from Massachusetts, is pictured on the rocky shore of his native state with the fish in the background representing the "codfish aristocracy" of New England.*

II-25 *Thomas Nast, "King Andy I. How He Will Look. What He Will Do,"* Harper's Weekly, *Nov. 3, 1886 (detail), wood engraving.*

II-25A *In the background of Nast's "King Andy I," those moving toward the chopping block include Charles Sumner, Henry Ward Beecher, Wendell Phillips and, at the end of the line, artist Nast himself.*

II-26 *G. Y. Coffin, "T. B. R. The Czar Is Dead. Long Live the Czar,"* detail from *"Some Random Opinions of a Recent Disturbance,"* Washington Post, *Nov. 15, 1894.*

II-26A *Another politician whom some cartoonists enjoyed depicting as a royal figure was Mark Hanna. Champe in* Up to Date, *June 27, 1896.*

THE NEW KING OF THE POLITICIANS—HANNA I.

II-27 *Edward Williams Clay (1799–1857), "The Rats Leaving a Falling House," 1831, lithograph. American Antiquarian Society, Worcester, Mass. See Parton, op. cit., p. 320.*
Mrs. Frances Trollope's observation appeared in her book, Domestic Manners of the Americans, *first published in 1832.*

II-28 *David Claypoole Johnston (1799–1865), "Symptoms of a Locked Jaw," 1834, lithograph. Johnston was known as "the American Cruikshank" because, in the manner of the English artist, he published an annual volume of his work called* Scraps. *For a brief autobiography, see William Dunlap,* A History of the Rise and Progress of the Arts of Design in the United States, *Frank K. Bayley and Charles E. Goodspeed, eds. (New York: Goodspeed, 1918), pp. 111–17.*

II-28A *A self-portrait from David Claypoole Johnston's* Phrenology Exemplified and Illustrated . . . Being Scraps No. 7 for the year 1837, *etching.*

III

Lithography and Early Magazines 1828-1865

1. See Harry T. Peters, *Currier & Ives: Printmaker to the American People* (Garden City, N.Y.: Doubleday, 1929, 1931), 2 vols.; Russell Crouse, *Mr. Currier & Mr. Ives* (Garden City, N.Y.: Doubleday, 1930); Frederic A. Conningham, *Currier & Ives* (Cleveland & New York: World, 1950).

III-1 *Louis Maurer (1832–1932), "Progressive Democracy—Prospect of a Smash Up," Currier & Ives, 1860, and photographs: III-1-1, Herschel V. Johnson (by Mathew Brady, courtesy Meserve Collection and Mrs. Philip B. Kunhardt); III-1-2, Stephen A. Douglas; III-1-3, James Buchanan; III-1-4, Abraham Lincoln (ambrotype by William Church, 1860); III-1-5, Hannibal Hamlin; III-1-6, John C. Breckinridge; III-1-7, Joseph Lane. See Joseph B. Bishop,* Our Political Drama *(New York: Scott-Thaw, 1904), p. 128.*

III-1A *1874, L. Prang & Co., Boston, "Lithographer," lithograph. At left, the limestone is being prepared for lithography by a worker who rubs it with a fine sand, which gives the stone a velvety surface. The artist (center) generally uses a crayon, though a pen or brush can be used if the ink is of the proper composition. At right, the stone has been placed in a press and is being coated with a greasy ink.*

2. Arthur Bartlett Maurice and Frederic Taber Cooper, *The History of the Nineteenth Century in Caricature, op. cit.,* pp. 143, 161.

3. See Joseph B. Bishop, "Early Political Caricature in America," *Century,* June, 1892, pp. 226–27. The Beard cartoon in a simplified form was also widely circulated on envelopes.

III-2 *Louis Maurer, "Storming the Castle, Old Abe on Guard," Currier & Ives, 1860, lithograph. Currier & Ives and other lithographic firms put out many more anti-Lincoln cartoons than those in his favor.*

III-3 *Louis Maurer, "The Republican Party Going to the Right House," Currier & Ives, 1860, lithograph.*

III-3A *Maurer drew a similar cartoon against Frémont in 1856. Lithograph, Currier & Ives.*

THE GREAT REPUBLICAN REFORM PARTY,
Calling on their Candidate.

4. *Vanity Fair*, June 6, 1860, p. 395.

III-4   *Anonymous, "Quakers and Franklin," 1764 (detail), engraving, Historical Society of Pennsylvania, Philadelphia.*

III-5   *"Hark from the Toombs, A Doleful Cry," wood engraving,* New York Illustrated News, *Jan. 19, 1861. Courtesy New-York Historical Society, New York City.*

III-6   *James A. Wales (1852–86), "More Fish Than He Can Land," lithograph,* Puck, *May 19, 1880.*

III-7   *F. Victor Gillam (d. 1920), "The Man with the Hoe," lithograph,* Judge, *Aug. 26, 1899.*

III-8   *"A War President," lithograph published by "Peter Smith" (Currier & Ives), 1848. Another pun on Cass's name during the 1848 Presidential campaign was "President (C)ass Beginning Operations," published by H. R. Robinson.*

III-9   *G. W. Carleton, "A Cass-us Ommissus," wood engraving,* Yankee Doodle, *I (1846).*

III-8A   *This detail of Cass as a gas bag is from "The Democratic Funeral of 1848," lithograph, published by Abel & Durang, Philadelphia.*

III-10 *"Brother, Beware. C-ass,"* *wood engraving,* The John-Donkey, *June 18, 1848. Widener Library, Harvard University.*

III-11 *H. R. Robinson, publisher, "Set-to Between the Champion Old Tip & the Swell Dutchman of Kinderhook—1836," lithograph, 1836. Van Buren's birthplace, Old Kinderhook, was translated by his Democratic organization into a lasting expression—"O.K."*

III-12 *James Baillie, publisher, "Political Cock Fighters," 1844, lithograph.*

III-13 *E. W. Clay, "Political Game of Brag. Shew of Hands," 1848, lithograph, published by Andrew Donnally.*

III-14 *Currier & Ives, publisher, "Great Footrace for the Presidential Purse ($100,000 and Pickings) over the* Union *Course 1852," 1852, lithograph.*

III-15 *Louis Maurer, "The National Game. Three 'Outs' and one 'Run.' Abraham winning the ball," 1860, lithograph, published by Currier & Ives. Although the National Association of Baseball Players was organized in 1858, the cartoon's title, "The National Game," probably was a lucky accident. The sport's terminology was already highly developed, yet it was still novel enough to be put in quotation marks—"home run," "foul," "put out," etc. Maurer, the punster, could not resist adding a skunk to illustrate which side was "skunked."*

III-16 *J. L. Magee, publisher, "A Little Game of Bagatelle Between Old Abe the Rail Splitter & Little Mac the Gunboat General," 1864, lithograph.*

III-17 *Honoré Daumier (1808-79), untitled, wood engraving,* Le Charivari, *July 3, 1838, Houghton Library, Harvard University. See Oliver W. Larkin,* Daumier: Man of His Time *(New York: McGraw-Hill, 1966), and Robert Rey,* Honoré Daumier *(New York: Harry N. Abrams, 1966).*

III-18 *Charles Philipon (1800–62), ["Sketched at the Trial of November 14"] (detail),* La Caricature, *Nov. 24, 1831, lithograph.*

5. J. Brander Matthews, "The Comic Literature of the United States," *The American Bibliopolist,* Aug., 1875.

III-19 *G. W. Carleton, cover, wood engraving,* Yankee Doodle, *May 1, 1847.*

III-20 *Felix O. C. Darley (1822–88), cover, wood engraving,* The John-Donkey, *Jan. 29, 1848.*

III-21 *Felix O. C. Darley, cover, wood engraving,* The Lantern, *Aug. 28, 1852.*

III-22 *Cover, wood engraving,* Momus, *May 26, 1860. The magazine began as a daily, which it remained for a month, after which it became a weekly.*

6. Orpheus C. Kerr, "The Mystery of Mr. E. Drood," *Punchinello,* June 25, 1870, p. 195.

7. See Arthur Penn, "The Growth of Caricature," *The Critic,* Feb. 25, 1882, pp. 49–50, and James Melvin Lee, "Punchinello and Its Cartoons," *Cartoons Magazine,* Aug., 1916, pp. 281–87.

8. *Uncle Sam,* June 21, 1879, p. 112. The magazine's chief political cartoonist was Palmer Cox (1840–1924), who later created the children's classic, *The Brownies.*

9. Richard Grant White, "Caricature and Caricaturists," *Harper's New Monthly Magazine,* Apr., 1862, p. 606.

10. "Carciature in America," *All the Year Round,* Sept. 28, 1878, p. 300.

11. Frank Linstow White, "Some American Caricaturists," *The Journalist,* Nov. 19, 1887, p. 6.

III-23 *Frank Bellew, "Reminiscences of Washington During the Inauguration," wood engraving,* The Lantern, *Mar. 19, 1853.*

III-22A *H. L. Stephens, cover, wood engraving,* Punchinello, *Apr. 16, 1870. Widener Library, Harvard University.*

III-23A *Frank Bellew, the most skillful political cartoonist working in the United States during the 1850s, as seen by Livingston Hopkins (1846–1927),* Wild Oats, *Nov. 12, 1874, wood engraving.*

III-24 *"This reminds me of a little joke," wood engraving,* Harper's Weekly, *Sept. 17, 1864. Lincoln's penchant for joke-telling is also satirized in "Running the Machine,"* Currier & Ives lithograph, 1864.

III-25 *Frank Bellew, "Long Abraham Lincoln a Little Longer," wood engraving,* Harper's Weekly, *Nov. 26, 1864.*

12. See James M. Scovel, "Recollections of Lincoln," *Lippincott's Magazine,* Feb., 1899, p. 278.

13. See Mitchell Mannering, "Historical Cartoons in American Politics," *National Magazine,* Nov., 1900, pp. 14, 16.

14. See Rufus Rockwell Wilson, *Lincoln in Caricature* (New York: Horizon, 1953), p. 180, and Dr. A. J. Volck, "Confederate War Etchings (1862–63)," *The Magazine of History* (Tarrytown, N.Y.: William Abbatt, 1917), p. 19.

15. Letter from A. J. Volck to Mrs. Gresham, Jan. 21, 1900, Confederate Museum, Richmond, Va.

16. See George C. Keidel, *Doctor Adalbert J. Volck, Caricaturist, and His Family, Personal Reminiscences,* typewritten copy in Library of Congress, n.d.

III-26 *Adalbert J. Volck (1828–1912), "Great American Tragedians, Comedians, and Clowns, and Rope Danzers in their Favorite Characters," 1861, etching. Secretary of the Treasury Salmon P. Chase is seen in the backdrop's window; the puppets are (foreground) Generals Frémont, Scott, and McClellan; Secretary of the Navy Gideon Welles (in the boat); General Ben Butler (sitting against the backdrop), and Secretary of War* Simon Cameron (*hanging from the backdrop*).

III-27 *"Master Abraham Lincoln Gets a New Toy," wood engraving,* Southern Illustrated News, *Feb. 28, 1863. Also see Richard Barksdale Harwell, "Confederate Anti-Lincoln Literature,"* Lincoln Herald, *Fall, 1951.*

III-28 *Matt Morgan, "Honest Abe's Rudder," wood engraving,* Fun (*London*), *May 9, 1863. See Walt McDougall, op. cit., pp. 64–5, and Alfred Trumble, "Satire, with Crayon and Penn,"* The Epoch, *June 13, 1890, pp. 299–300.*

III-29 *John Tenniel, "Abe Lincoln's Last Card; or, Rouge-et-Noir," wood engraving,* Punch, or The London Charivari, *Oct. 18, 1862.*

III-30 *John Tenniel, "Britannia Sympathises with Columbia," wood engraving,* Punch, or The London Charivari, *May 6, 1865.*

IV

Magazines 1866-1896

IV-1   *Thomas Nast, "Th. Nast, April—21—84," Pen and ink drawing.*

IV-2   *Thomas Nast, self-portrait, etching, 1892.*

IV-3   *Frank Bellew, "Mixing Day at Harpers—Making Mud to Fling at Greeley," Fifth Avenue Journal, 1872, in Albert Bigelow Paine, op. cit.*

1. J. V. Whitaker, "American Caricaturists, IV—Thomas Nast," *Leisure Hour,* Dec. 16, 1876, p. 810.

IV-4   *Thomas Nast, "Compromise with the South," wood engraving,* Harper's Weekly, Sept. 3, 1864.

IV-4A   *The "Compromise with the South" that appeared in* Harper's Weekly *was only half of Nast's original design. Many years later he resketched it for Arthur Bartlett Maurice, "Thomas Nast and His Cartoons,"* The Bookman, *Mar., 1902. Nast usually used his wife as the model for Columbia (seen here kneeling at the grave).*

2. Rufus Rockwell Wilson, *op. cit.*, p. xv.

IV-5   *Thomas Nast, "The 'Brains,' " wood engraving,* Harper's Weekly, *Oct. 21, 1871. The Mariners Museum, Newport News, Va.*

IV-6   *Thomas Nast, "The Tammany Tiger Loose—'What are you going to do about it?' " Wood engraving,* Harper's Weekly, *Nov. 11, 1871. The Mariners Museum, Newport News, Va.*

IV-6A   *John Tenniel, "The British Lion's Vengeance on the Bengal Tiger," wood engraving,* Punch, or The London Charivari, *Aug. 22, 1857. The Tammany Tiger owes an artistic debt to* Punch's *Tenniel, whose important series on the Cawnpore Mutiny of 1857 was studied by young Nast.*

IV-7 *Thomas Nast, "Group of Vultures Waiting for the Storm to 'Blow Over'—'Let Us Prey,'"* wood engraving, Harper's Weekly, *Sept. 23, 1871. The Mariners Museum, Newport News, Va.*

IV-8 *Thomas Nast, "The Only Thing They Respect or Fear,"* wood engraving, Harper's Weekly, *Oct. 21, 1871. The Mariners Museum, Newport News, Va.*

IV-9 *Thomas Nast, "Something That Did Blow Over—November 7, 1871,"* wood engraving, Harper's Weekly, *Nov. 25, 1871. The Mariners Museum, Newport News, Va.*

IV-10 *Thomas Nast, "The American River Ganges,"* wood engraving, Harper's Weekly, *Sept. 30, 1871. The Mariners Museum, Newport News, Va.*

IV-10A *One of Keppler's many representations of his hostility toward the Catholic Church, "Pope Leo XIII, a Physiognomical Study,"* lithograph, Puck, *Apr. 24, 1878.*

IV-11 *Frederick Opper, "Tommy Sees Snakes Again.—A T.-Nast-y Cartoon," wood engraving,* Wild Oats, *June 14, 1876. Courtesy of The New-York Historical Society, New York City.*

IV-11A *"Thomas Nast at work again," lithograph,* Puck, *June 4, 1879. A well-labeled spoof of a "typical" Nast cartoon. Rivals also suggested that Nast did not think up his own ideas. Walt McDougall, who loved any bit of malicious gossip about a fellow cartoonist, wrote that "his cartoons were really originated by a clever brother-in-law . . . ," op cit., p. 118; Paine's biography says that Nast's wife was responsible for many "of the terse and telling legends beneath his cartoons," op cit., p. 121. But stories* of this sort were told about Daumier, Keppler, Davenport, and almost every other cartoonist who rose above the herd. *More probable is W. A. Rogers' assessment: "It has been said that some mysterious person or persons furnished him [Nast] with the brilliant ideas which he executed with such strength and vigor, but I never heard a particle of evidence to support the story, and to one who knew him it seems absurd."* A World Worth While *(New York: Harper, 1922), p. 284.*

3. Arthur Penn, "The Growth of Caricature," *The Critic,* Feb. 25, 1882, p. 49. Arthur Penn has been said to be a pen name of Brander Matthews.

4. See Art Young, *Art Young: His Life and Times* (New York: Sheridan House, 1939), p. 122.

IV-12 *Thomas Nast, "The New Organ-(we beg the 'Tribune's pardon)-ization on Its 'New Departure'—Any Thing to Get Votes," wood engraving, Harper's Weekly, June 8, 1872. The organ grinder–monkey relationship has been a common analogy for political cartoonists:*

IV-12A *Frank Bellew, "The Whig Organ Exhibiting a Specimen of Feathery Tribe," wood engraving, The Lantern, Aug. 28, 1852. Ironically, here Greeley is the organ-grinder; Winfield Scott is the monkey.*

IV-12B *Charles Nelan, untitled, Scripps-McRae League, 1896. Thomas Francis Bayard, the U.S. Ambassador to Great Britain, was under attack for his supposedly pro-British sympathies.*

IV-12C *Emil Flohri (1869–1938), "Croker and His Monkey," lithograph, Judge, Oct. 6, 1900.*

IV-13 Thomas Nast, "Let us clasp hands over the bloody chasm," wood engraving, Harper's Weekly, Sept. 21, 1872.

IV-14 Thomas Nast, "We are on the home stretch," wood engraving, Harper's Weekly, Nov. 2, 1872.

IV-15 Thomas Nast, "Volcanoes Cannot Stop Thomas Nast," New York Herald, May 18, 1902.

IV-16 Joseph Keppler (1838–94), "A Mid-Summer Day's Dream," lithograph, Puck, Aug. 10, 1881. For another amusing self-portrait of Keppler, see "The Return of 'The Prodigal Father' to the 'Puck' Office," Puck, Oct. 10, 1883.

IV-17 Joseph Keppler, "A Stir in the Roost," lithograph, Puck, Mar., 1877. The "chickens" include Whitelaw Reid, editor of the New York Tribune; Frank Leslie; George Jones, co-founder of The New York Times; James Gordon Bennett, director of the New York Herald; Charles A. Dana, owner-editor of the New York Sun; Thomas Nast; and William Cullen Bryant, editor of the New York Evening Post.

5. See Eugene Zimmerman, "Rambles in Cartoondom," Cartoons Magazine, Apr., 1916, p. 577.

6. See the first-rate work by Draper Hill, "What Fools These Mortals Be!" A Study of the Work of Joseph Keppler—Founder of Puck (unpublished A.B. thesis, Harvard College, 1957), p. 106.

7. Joseph B. Bishop, Our Political Drama, op. cit., p. 156.

IV-18 "The 13-15-14 Puzzle in the Senate," New York Tribune, Mar. 18, 1880.

IV-19 James A. Wales, "15-14-13-The Great Presidential Puzzle,"

lithograph, Puck, Mar. 17, 1880. For other cartoons (by Opper) based on the 15-puzzle, which was the rage of the day, see Puck, Mar. 10, 1880.

8. Puck, June 9, 1880, p. 238.

IV-20 Joseph Keppler, "Forbidding the Banns," lithograph, Puck, Aug. 25, 1880. In the 1940s and '50s, Sam Cobean drew a justly famous series of New Yorker cartoons on the same unwed-mother theme. See The Cartoons of Cobean (New York: Harper, 1952).

IV-21 Joseph Keppler, "The Democratic Samson and the Republican Philistines," lithograph, Puck, Sept. 15, 1880.

9. Arthur Bartlett Maurice and Frederic T. Cooper, The History of the Nineteenth Century in Caricature, op. cit., p. 233.

10. John J. Ingalls, "Cartoons: What They Are and What They Do," in Cartoons by Davenport (New York: De Witt, 1898), no page numbers.

11. Harry Thruston Peck, "Here and There," The Bookman, Oct., 1900, p. 117.

12. William J. Arkell, Old Friends and Some Acquaintances, op. cit., p. 76. For other statements of the Tattooed Man's genesis, see Albert B. Paine, op. cit., p. 502; Maurice and Cooper, op. cit., p. 277; James L. Ford, Forty-Odd Years in the Literary Shop (New York: Dutton, 1921), p. 299; New York Journal, Jan. 18, 1896, p. 6.

IV-22 Bernard Gillam (1856–96), "Phryne Before the Chicago Tribunal," lithograph, Puck, June 4, 1884. Among those watching Whitelaw Reid unveil the tattooed Blaine are (seated from right to left) George William Curtis of Harper's Weekly, former Secretary

of State William Evarts, Carl Schurz, and young Theodore Roosevelt. Behind Roosevelt are Senator John Sherman of Ohio (white beard) and Senator John Logan of Illinois (black beard). Grant Hamilton later tried to apply the Tattooed Man theme to "Boss" Richard Croker of Tammany, but the idea had had its vogue and failed to catch on the second time around. See "A Christmas Bath," Judge, Dec. 29, 1900.

IV-23 Joseph Keppler, "The Royal Tattoo," wood engraving, Frank Leslie's Budget of Fun, Feb., 1875.

IV-24 Joseph Keppler, "Auch eine Tätowirte," lithograph, Puck, German ed., Nov., 1876. Courtesy New York Public Library.

IV-25 Frank Beard (1842–1905), "Another Voice for Cleveland," lithograph, Judge, Sept. 27, 1884. For his religious cartoons, see Frank Beard, Fifty Great Cartoons (Chicago: Ram's Horn Press, 1899).

IV-26 Joseph Keppler, "The Raven," lithograph, Puck, Aug. 13, 1890.

IV-27 Joseph Keppler, "Where Is He?" lithograph, Puck, Nov. 16, 1892.

IV-28 James A. Wales, "The Two Political Dromios," lithograph, Judge, Oct. 29, 1881. For Wales's background, see Henry C. Williamson, "Back in the Past, III," Cartoons Magazine, Mar., 1913, p. 178.

13. William J. Arkell, op. cit., pp. 73–4. Also see Henry C. Williamson, "Back in the Past, IV," Cartoons Magazine, Apr., 1913, p. 242.

IV-29 Bernard Gillam, "Benjamin

—'Where Am I At?'" lithograph, Judge, *Nov. 19, 1892.*

14. James Montgomery Flagg, *Roses and Buckshot, op. cit.,* p. 44.

IV-30 *Grant Hamilton, "Lost!" lithograph,* Judge, *Sept. 15, 1900.*

IV-31 *F. Victor Gillam, "Don Quixote Bryan Meets Disaster in his Fight Against Judge's 'Full Dinner-Pail,'" lithograph,* Judge, *Nov. 10, 1900.*

IV-32 *John Ames Mitchell (1845–1918), untitled, illustration for his article "Contemporary American Caricature,"* Scribner's Magazine, *Dec., 1889.*

IV-33 *William H. Walker (1871–1938), "J. A. M., As Seen by a Contributor,"* The Book News Monthly, *Mar., 1912.*

IV-34 *Louis Maurer, "An Heir to the Throne, or The Next Republican Candidate," 1860, lithograph, published by Currier & Ives.*

IV-35 *"The Coming Men!" wood engraving,* Frank Leslie's Illustrated Newspaper, *Feb. 28, 1863. See* Yankee Doodle, *I (1846–47), p. 278, for another cartoon based on Tom Thumb.*

IV-35A *Siamese twins on exhibition at Barnum's Museum inspired a cartoon by H. L. Stephens, "Wonderful Surgical Operation Performed by Doct. Lincoln on the Political Chang and Eng,"* Vanity Fair, *Nov., 1860, wood engraving.*

IV-36 J. H. Howard, "I knew him, Horatio; a fellow of infinite jest," 1864, wood engraving.

IV-37 Bernard Gillam, "The Path of Duty," lithograph (detail), Puck, Dec. 28, 1881.

The use of Shakespearean themes, of course, has not been limited to Hamlet:

IV-37A President Jackson as Lady Macbeth. E. W. Clay, 1837.

IV-37B President Johnson as Julius Caesar. Herblock, Washington Post, June 10, 1966.

IV-38 Frederick Opper, "The Latest Version," lithograph, Puck, Apr. 11, 1894. Many politicians have been amused by the way they have been depicted by the cartoonists, but Richard Croker (1841–1922) must win some kind of award in this category. He published a handsomely bound volume, its cover stamped in gold, Political Cartoons Gathered by Their Target—Richard Croker (New York: W. P. Mitchell, 1901?). Its dedication reads: "To my friends whose confidence was unwavering when the shafts were barbed with malice and falsehoods, and when wit or humor fashioned the arrow, mingled their laughter with mine, this collection from leading American Cartoonists is offered."

IV-39 Homer Davenport, "Hannalet, Prince of $ Mark in the Modern Graveyard Scene," New York Journal and Advertiser, July 6, 1899.

IV-40 Joseph Keppler, Jr. (1872–1956), "Tedlet's Soliloquy," lithograph, Puck, Oct. 30, 1907.

15. Oliver Herford, Confessions of a Caricaturist (New York: Scribner's, 1917), p. 34.

IV-41 Joseph Keppler, "A Harmless Explosion," lithograph, Puck, May 25, 1881.

IV-41A Thomas Nast, "Now then, butt away!," wood engraving, Harper's Weekly, Nov. 22, 1879 (detail), Conkling as goat.

IV-41B Thomas Nast, "Borrowed plumes—Mr. Jack Daw Conkling," wood engraving, Harper's Weekly, Dec. 20, 1879 (detail), Conkling as jackdaw.

IV-41C Thomas Nast, "Let him alone—now he's come home," wood engraving, Harper's Weekly, June 4, 1881, Conkling as lamb.

IV-42   *Francis G. Attwood
(1865–1900), "I am hungry! Please
drop a nomination in the hat,"* Life,
*June 19, 1884. Attwood first began
caricaturing Butler while at Harvard,
where in 1876 he was a founder of
the* Lampoon. *In an era when
cartoonists tended to draw on a
grand scale, he was a miniaturist
whose delicate double-page designs
for* Life *sometimes contained as
many as 150 complete figures. See
Lloyd McK. Garrison, "The Work
of a Great Cartoonist,"* Century,
Sept., 1900, and Francis G. Attwood,
Attwood's Pictures, An Artist's
History of the Last Ten Years of
the Nineteenth Century (*New York:
Life Publishing Co., 1900*).

IV-43   *Mirs, " 'Czar' Reed is
Ready," lithograph,* The Verdict,
*Jan. 2, 1899. For Reed wearing a
crown also see Charles Nelan, "Our
Great Objector," New York* Herald,
*Feb. 23, 1898, and Will E. Chapin
of the Los Angeles* Times *in*
Cartoons of Will E. Chapin (*Los
Angeles: Times-Mirror Printing,
1899*).

16. John Ames Mitchell,
"Contemporary American
Caricature," *op. cit.,* p. 35.

17. Fairfax Downey, *op. cit.,* p. 44.

18. See Draper Hill, *op. cit.,* pp.
35–7.

19. James L. Ford, *op. cit.,* p. 298.

PLATES AND NOTES

Newspapers
1884-1968

V-1   *John Wesley Jarvis
(1780–1840), "The Death of the
Embargo with all its 'Restrictive
Energies,' " metal cut, New York*
Evening Post, *Apr. 25, 1814. Murrell
called portrait painter Jarvis "a
reckless, extravagant, bustling,
guzzling fellow."*

1. See Richard O'Connor, *The
Scandalous Mr. Bennett* (Garden
City, N.Y.: Doubleday, 1962), pp.
68–70.

V-1A *J. Campbell Cory (b. 1867), "James Gordon Bennett," lithograph,* Bee, *May 25, 1898. Widener Library, Harvard University. For biographical information on the colorful Cory, who was also publisher of the short-lived* Bee, *see B. O. Flower, "J. Campbell Cory, Cartoonist,"* The Arena, *Jan., 1906, and* Cartoons Magazine, *May, 1915, p. 796. Charles Kendrick also drew an interesting caricature of James Gordon Bennett in* Chic, *supplement to issue of Feb. 22, 1881.*

V-2 *"The Federal Edifice," metal cut,* Massachusetts Centinel, *Aug. 2, 1788. This series was meant to be more than an illustrated graph to show the progress of state ratification of the Federal Constitution. The cartoons were making a pro-Constitution argument by turning the states into pillars.*

V-3 *Frank Bellew, "The Modern Laocoon," wood engraving, New York* Daily Graphic, *April 25, 1874. New England Deposit Library.*

V-4 *Walt McDougall, "The Royal Feast of Belshazzar Blaine and the Money Kings," New York* World, *Oct. 30, 1884.*

V-5 *Leon Barritt (1852–1938), "The Big Type War of the Yellow Kids," lithograph,* Vim, *June 29, 1898. Barritt was also the publisher of* The Evening Sky Map, *an astronomical magazine. For other cartoons of Hearst and Pulitzer see J. Campbell Cory,* Bee, *June 8, 1898, and J. H. Donahey, "Why Go to Africa for Big Game?"* Cleveland Plain Dealer, *Jan. 20, 1909. Throughout the nineteenth century, cartoonists were almost as apt to caricature newspapermen as politicians. Horace Greeley may have been the most satirized public figure of his time, even before he left the editorship of the New York* Tribune *to run for President; James Gordon Bennett, Sr., founder of the New York* Herald, *was almost as popular a subject.*

V-5A *"See Porcupine, in Colours Just Portray'd," 1799, engraving. Courtesy Historical Society of Pennsylvania, Philadelphia. One of the better eighteenth-century cartoons was devoted to writer-publisher William Cobbett, known as "Peter Porcupine," who is shown libeling liberal statesmen while the Devil and the British Lion look on approvingly.*

V-5B *H. L. Stephens, "Editorial Washing-Day in New-York," wood engraving,* Punchinello, *May 28, 1870. From left to right: Manton Marble, New York* World; *Horace Greeley, New York* Tribune; *(background) Hugh J. Hastings, New York* Commercial Advertiser; *George Jones, The New York* Times; *(background) Theodore Tilton, New York* Independent; *John Russell Young, New York* Standard; *Charles Dana, New York* Sun.

V-5C *J. S. Pughe (1871–1909), in "If. The Inaugural Dinner at the White House," shows "President" Hearst celebrating with the characters that appeared in his newspapers' comic strips. Lithograph in* Puck, *June 29, 1904.*

V-6 *Grant Hamilton, "The Spanish Brute," lithograph, Judge, July 9, 1898.*

V-7 *Blanco Coris, untitled, Blanco y Negro (Madrid), Feb. 19, 1898. Courtesy The Memorial Library, University of Wisconsin, Madison.*

V-7A *Some American cartoonists had some fun by turning the Spaniards' "Yankee Pig" theme against them. Charles Bartholomew (1869–1949), "The Little King of Spain and the Yankee Pig," Minneapolis Journal, July 12, 1898. Pen and ink drawing. See Cartoons of the War of 1898 with Spain (Chicago: Belford, Middlebrook & Co., 1898).*

V-8 *William H. Walker, "Our Expansive Uncle," Life, Dec. 28, 1899. See "Life's Family Album, Wm. H. Walker," Life, June 22, 1911, p. 1220.*

2. Thomas Craven, *Cartoon Cavalcade, op. cit.,* p. 11.

V-9 *Frederick Opper, "Willie and His Papa," New York Evening Journal, June 27, 1900. The series began on May 30, 1900.*

V-10 *Frederick Opper, "The M'Kinley Minstrels," New York Journal and Advertiser, Feb. 19, 1901.*

V-11 *Frederick Opper, "Nursery Rhymes for Infant Industries: An Alphabet of Joyous Trusts—No. 5," New York American and Journal, Sept. 27, 1902.*

3. See Homer Davenport, *The Dollar or the Man?* (Boston: Small, Maynard, 1900), p. 7.

4. "The Personal Narrative of Homer Davenport, An Interview with the Famous Cartoonist," *The Pacific Monthly,* Dec., 1905, p. 520.

5. See Homer Davenport, *My Quest of the Arab Horse* (New York: B. W. Dodge, 1909).

V-12 *Homer Davenport, "Mark Hanna as he is and as Davenport made him," New York Journal, Nov. 8, 1896. See Homer Davenport, "The Gentle Art of Making the Wicked Squirm," New York Journal and Advertiser, Apr. 16, 1899.*

V-13 *Homer Davenport, "I am Confident the Working Men Are with us," New York Journal, Oct. 8, 1896. See Stephen Hess, "The Making of the President, 1896,"* The Nineties *(New York: American Heritage, 1967); also Julia B. Foraker,* I Would Live It Again

(*New York: Harper, 1932*), *pp. 91–2.*

V-14 *Homer Davenport, "A Man of Mark!" New York* Journal, *Aug. 4, 1896. See Margaret Leech,* In the Days of McKinley (*New York: Harper, 1959*), *pp. 76, 619. Hanna was really an enlightened employer who had said of George Pullman's refusal to arbitrate the railroad strike of 1894: "A man who won't meet his men half-way is a God-damn fool!" Yet Davenport so popularized another view of Hanna that when, during a campaign speech, he offered $100 to find a dollar mark on his suit, a man shouted: "Of course we can't see 'em. They're branded on yer hide."*

V-15 *Homer Davenport, "The New Anthem at Philadelphia," New York* Journal and Advertiser, *June 16, 1900. The Republican National Convention was then being held at Philadelphia. The cartoon was later reproduced in Davenport's* The Dollar or the Man? *with the caption, "Mark, Wouldn't it be Great for the Standard Oil Dinner Bell!"*

V-16 *Homer Davenport, "Wall Street Wishes a New Guardian of the Treasury," New York* Journal, *Sept. 1, 1896.*

V-17 *Homer Davenport, "The Head of the Procession Coming Out of Wall Street," New York* Journal and Advertiser, *Nov. 4, 1900. Pen and ink drawing.*

6. John T. McCutcheon, "Roosevelt as Cartoon Material," *Evening Post,* Mar. 13, 1909, p. 24.

7. For Theodore Roosevelt's cartoons, see Corinne R. Robinson, *My Brother, Theodore Roosevelt* (New York: Scribner's, 1921).

V-18 *J. K. Bryans, "What May Happen to Teddy If He Doesn't Stop Making Speeches About Himself,"* Texas Siftings, *Mar. 14, 1896.*

V-19 *E. G. Lutz, "We Wouldn't Say 'Blockhead,'"* Satire, *July 20, 1912.*

V-20 *Camillus Kessler, "The Gargoyle," St. Louis* Times, *1912, reprinted in* Cartoons Magazine, *June, 1912.*

V-21 *William C. Morris (1874–1940), "President Roosevelt and the Third Term. Is This a Prophecy?" Spokane (Washington)* Spokesman-Review, *Apr. 11, 1907.*

V-22 *A. W. Brewerton (1881–1960), "Where Teddy's Announcement Caused Joy," Atlanta* Journal, *Feb. 27, 1912.*

V-23 *Clifford K. Berryman, "Drawing the Line in Mississippi," detail from "The Passing Show," Washington* Post, *Nov. 16, 1902.*

V-23A *Clifford K. Berryman, self-portrait with "Teddy Bear,"* Cartoons Magazine, *June, 1912, p. 37.*

V-23B *Robert W. Satterfield, untitled,* Cartoons Magazine, *Feb., 1913, p. 90. This little fellow by Satterfield of the Central Press Association was also inspired by Roosevelt's Mississippi bear hunt and probably came before Berryman's bear. But Satterfield lost his place in history to Berryman because he had the misfortune of naming his animal "Mose" instead of "Teddy." See Raymond Gros,* T. R. in Cartoon *(Akron: Saalfield Publishing, 1910), p. vii.*

V-24 *Homer Davenport, "Uncle Sam: 'After all is said and done, he's still Good Enough for Me,'" 1904 campaign poster based on a cartoon that originally appeared in the New York* Evening Mail. *Davenport drew a sequel to this famous cartoon during the 1908 campaign; called "The Important Introduction," it showed T. R. introducing Uncle Sam to William Howard Taft.*

V-25 *Charles Macauley (1871–1934), "He's Good Enough for Me," New York* World, *Mar. 10, 1912. This was not the only take-off on the Davenport cartoon; Bill Nye of the Louisville* Courier-Journal *drew one in which Uncle Sam says to T. R., "Not good enough for me." Macauley did outstanding work for the* World *(1904–14), but Ralph Pulitzer fired him from his $250-a-week position because of the cartoonist's active participation in a New York City mayorality campaign. (He then successfully sued Pulitzer for breach of contract.) Ironically, Macauley later was to win a Pulitzer Prize (1930, Brooklyn* Eagle).

V-26 *Joseph Keppler, Jr., "The Courtship of Bill Taft," lithograph,* Puck, *Apr. 24, 1907.*

V-27 *John T. McCutcheon, "The Presidential Holiday: He Arrives in 'San Antone' to Attend a Reunion of the Rough Riders," Chicago* Daily Tribune, *Apr. 6, 1905, reprinted in* The Mysterious Stranger and Other Cartoons *(New York: McClure, Phillips, 1905). See John T. McCutcheon,* Drawn from Memory *(Indianapolis & New York: Bobbs-Merrill, 1950), p. 199.*

V-28 *John T. McCutcheon, "The Mysterious Stranger," Chicago* Daily Tribune, *Nov. 10, 1904.*

V-28A *McCutcheon's marriage in 1917 caused his friend Clare Briggs (1875–1930) to picture him as "The Mysterious Stranger." Courtesy Mrs. John T. McCutcheon.*
The Tribune *announced McCutcheon's death in 1949 with an eight-column banner headline across its front page. He had been with the paper for forty-three years, and Chicagoans had come to think of him as one of the city's natural resources.*

V-29 *Jay N. Darling (1876–1962), "The Long, Long Trail," New York* Tribune, *Jan. 10, 1919.*

V-30 *Jay N. Darling, "Gone to Join the Mysterious Caravan," Des Moines* Register, *Jan. 11, 1917.*

V-31 *William A. Rogers (1854–1931), "In the Grasp of the Cartoon Trust," New York* Herald, *Jan. 14, 1914.*

V-32 *"Little Billy Bryan Chasing Butterflies," lithograph,* Judge, *Oct. 17, 1896.*

V-33 *Eugene Zimmerman (1862–1933), " 'Trade Follows the Flag,' but Democrats Follow the Fool," lithograph,* Judge, *July 7, 1900.*

V-34 *Charles Bartholomew, "Temptation," Minneapolis* Journal, *July 4, 1902. For biographical information on "Bart," see B. D. Flower, "A Pioneer Newspaper Cartoonist,"* The Arena, *Jan., 1905.*

V-35 *Nelson Harding (1879–1947), "Sunshine and Shadow," Brooklyn* Eagle, *Jan. 18, 1908. Harding considered himself a "Bull Mooser" and had actually served under Roosevelt at San Juan Hill. He won the Pulitzer Prize twice for the Brooklyn* Eagle *(1927 and 1928) and then switched to the New York* Journal, *where he ended his long career in 1945. See Gerald W. Johnson,* The Lines Are Drawn *(Philadelphia & New York: Lippincott, 1958), pp. 48–59, and Nelson Harding,* The Political Campaign of 1912 in Cartoons *(Brooklyn: Brooklyn* Daily Eagle, *1912), p. 14.*

V-36 *Robert Minor (1884–1952), "Another Farewell Tour?" St. Louis* Post-Dispatch, *reprinted in* Cartoons Magazine, *July, 1912.*

V-37 *Oscar Cesare (1885–1948),*
"Dropping the Pilot," New York
Sun, June 11, 1915. His model was
the classic Tenniel cartoon of the
Kaiser dismissing Bismarck.

DROPPING THE PILOT.

V-37A *Sir John Tenniel,*
"Dropping the Pilot," wood
engraving, Punch, or the London
Charivari, *Mar. 29, 1890. William*
H. Walker in Life, *Dec. 26, 1918,*
used the same theme with the title,
"Dropping the Pirate," the
"pirate/pilot" being the Kaiser.

V-37B *A more recent event—the*
defeat of Winston Churchill's
Conservative Party after World War
II—prompted another variation on
the Tenniel drawing. Daniel Bishop,
(1900–59) "Dropping the Pilot,"
St. Louis Star-Times, *July 27, 1945.*

V-38 Rollin Kirby (1875–1952), "Gathering Data for the Tennessee Trial," New York World, May 19, 1925.

V-39 William A. Rogers, "He Had Expected to Find the President Alone," New York Herald, June 3, 1915. Inspired by the German Ambassador's audience with President Wilson after the Lusitania was sunk on May 7, 1915.

V-40 William A. Rogers, "What We're Going to do to those Neutrals Will Break our Tender Hearts," New York Herald, Jan. 7, 1917. The "pirates" in the cartoon are Von Tirpitz (left) and the Kaiser. For biographical information on Rogers, see his memoirs, A World Worth While (New York: Harper, 1922), and "W. A. Rogers: The Cartoonists of Civic Integrity," The Arena, Apr., 1906. For a collection of his pro-war cartoons, see William A. Rogers, America's Black and White Book (New York: Cupples & Leon, 1917).

V-41 William A. Rogers, "Another case of wiping hands on the American flag," New York Herald, Feb. 21, 1917.

V-42 Luther D. Bradley (1853–1917), "Out?" Chicago Daily News, July 30, 1914.

V-43 Luther D. Bradley, "Just for Good Measure," Chicago Daily News, Sept. 28, 1915.

V-44 Luther D. Bradley, "The Final Answer?" Chicago Daily News, Jan. 4, 1917. For an excellent biographical sketch of the artist, see Henry J. Smith in Luther D. Bradley, Cartoons by Bradley (Chicago: Rand McNally, 1917).

V-45 Louis Raemaekers (1869–1956), "Kultur Has Passed Here," from Raemaekers' Cartoons (Garden City, N.Y.: Doubleday, Page, 1917). Also see Lewis R. Freeman, "Louis Raemaekers and His War Cartoons," The Outlook, Mar. 15, 1916, Mme. Bernardini Sjoestedt, "Louis Raemaekers, The Arch Enemy of the Kaiser," Cartoons Magazine, May, 1916; The War Cartoons of Louis Raemaekers (New York: Brown Robertson, 1917); The War Cartoons of Louis Raemaekers, A Catalogue (New York: Land & Water, 1917).

8. See Oscar Cesare, One Hundred Cartoons (Boston: Small, Maynard, 1917). On the question of the cartoonist's role in wartime, see Lyman Abbott, "Cartoons and Caricatures in War Times," The Outlook, Nov. 8, 1916, and William Murrell, "Cartooning in Wartime America," Art News, Apr. 1-14, 1943.

V-46 Charles H. Sykes (1882–1942), "We Can, We Must, and We Will!" Philadelphia Evening Public Ledger, reprinted in Cartoons Magazine, June, 1918. See "Sykes of the Philadelphia Public Ledger," Cartoons Magazine, July, 1913, p. 65, and "Cartoonists as They See Themselves," The Literary Digest, Dec. 23, 1933, p. 10.

V-47 Raymond O. Evans (1887–1954), "The Cornerstone," Baltimore American, Aug. 14, 1918, reprinted in George J. Hecht, The War in Cartoons (New York: Dutton, 1919). Evans worked for the Baltimore American from 1912 to 1921 and for the Columbus (Ohio) Dispatch, 1922 until his death. See James E. Pollard, "You Can't Draw on Face Value Alone," The Quill, Sept., 1941.

V-48 Paul Fung (1898–1944), "The Sweetheart of the Allies," Seattle Post-Intelligencer, Sept. 9, 1918. Courtesy Seattle Public Library, Seattle, Washington. See Jack Bechdolt, "Fung, The Only Chinese-American Cartoonist in Captivity," Cartoons Magazine, July, 1916.

9. For an interesting anthology of the magazine, see William L. O'Neill, ed., Echoes of Revolt: The Masses 1911-1917 (Chicago: Quadrangle, 1966). See also Frederick J. Hoffman, Charles Allen, and Carolyn F. Ulrich, The Little Magazine (Princeton: Princeton University Press, 1946).

10. See B. O. Flower, "Ryan Walker: A Cartoonist of Social Protest," The Arena, Apr., 1905.

11. See Lloyd Goodrich, John Sloan (New York: Macmillan, 1952), pp. 41–7.

V-49 Boardman Robinson (1876–1952), "Europe, 1916," The Masses, Oct., 1916. See "The American Cartoon," The Independent, Jan. 23, 1913; Boardman Robinson, Ninety-Three Drawings (Colorado Springs: Colorado Springs Fine Arts Center, 1937) and Cartoons on the War (New York: Dutton, 1915).

V-50 Robert Minor, "Army Medical Examiner: 'At last a perfect soldier!'" The Masses, July, 1916. See Robert Minor, "Cartoons, The Slang of Art," Cartoons Magazine, Mar., 1913, p. 135.

V-50A *Art Young (1866–1943), draws his friend Robert Minor in* Good Morning, *May 10–15, 1921. When Minor left the St. Louis* Post-Dispatch *in 1913 his cartoonist's chair was taken over by a young man named Daniel R. Fitzpatrick, whose style obviously owed a debt to his predecessor.*

V-51 *Art Young, "System,"* Good Morning, *June 12, 1919. See Art Young,* On My Way *(New York: Liveright, 1928),* The Best of Art Young *(New York: Vanguard, 1936), and* Art Young, His Life and Times, *op. cit.*

Bum Biographies -- No. 2

Like the late Jack London, Robert **Minor**, cartoonist, writer and speaker, looks like a rough-neck. When he talks, however, it is as if he thought a reporter for posterity were listening in and his words and sentences are formed with precision, and are grammatical enough to suggest that a good college professor was lost to the world when Bob joined the proletarian movement.

Speaking of sentences, Minor was sentenced by an Allied military court in the occupational zone in Southern Germany, for alleged distribution of Russian propaganda. He writes well and can make cartoons that are masterpieces of technical simplicity and force. He is the son of a popular San Antonio, Texas, judge, is thirty-seven years old and has had a lot of experience for a young man.

V-51A *Peggy Bacon (b. 1895), "Portrait of Art Young," in* Off with Their Heads! *(New York: McBride, 1934). Peggy Bacon said that Art Young's face was "illuminated like an old manuscript with a scroll-work of humorous wrinkles." It was also written that he "looks like an angel much the worse for wear and tear."*

12. See *Red Cartoons from the Daily Worker, The Worker's Monthly and the Liberator* (Chicago: Daily Worker Publishing Co., 1926), and *1929 Red Cartoons Reprinted from the Daily Worker* (New York: Comprodaily Publishing Co., 1929).

V-52 *William Gropper (b. 1897), "Decorating the Greatest Hero,"* Good Morning, *June 12, 1919. See* William Gropper, *Gropper (New York: A.C.A. Gallery, 1938) and* Editor & Publisher, *Aug. 10, 1935, p. 10.*

V-53 *Alfred Frueh (b. 1880), "Society Note from Moscow,"* Good Morning, *May 15, 1919.*

V-54 *Charles G. Bush (1842–1909), "Sorosis 1869," wood engraving,* Harper's Weekly, *May 15, 1869. Courtesy Mariners Museum, Newport News, Va. Bush's delicate technique was said to be "almost like painting with a pen." Besides* Harper's Weekly, *his work often appeared in the New York* Evening Telegram *and* Life; *and he ended his long career with the New York* World. *See "A Master Cartoonist,"* The World's Work, *Feb., 1901.*

V-55 *James H. Donahey (1875–1949), "Gen. Rosalie Jones Crossing the Delaware,"* Cleveland Plain Dealer, *Feb. 15, 1913. Donahey, whose work appeared in the* Plain Dealer *for fifty years, was in the McCutcheon tradition of gentle, rurally-oriented wit; as with William Ireland of Columbus, large offers could not lure him from Ohio. See Russell H. Reeves, "Cartoons Will Outweigh the Written Word,"* The Quill, *July, 1941.*

V-56 *John Held, Jr. (1889–1958), "The Only Way,"* Judge, *Nov. 9, 1912. Held, of course, is best known for his "flapper," that pert and frisky baby-doll who epitomized the 1920s. His cartoons in praise of bootleg gin and jazz bands were a constant feature of* Life *and the other mass-circulation magazines. A second style, which he drew for the early issues of* The New Yorker *as a parody of the Victorian era, was a melodramatic, deliberately crude imitation of early wood engravings. Held's frivolity no longer seemed appropriate during the Depression 1930s, and, rather than change his style, the artist turned his energy to horse breeding, ceramics, and wrought-iron sculpture. See Walt Reed, ed.,* The Illustrator in America, 1900–1960s *(New York: Reinhold, 1966), p. 92.*

V-57 *Henry (Hy) Mayer (1868–1954), "Touch me not, I'm a lady!"* The New York Times, *Dec. 8, 1912. Mayer was known for his versatility and cosmopolitan approach. While he was drawing "Impressions of the Passing Show" for* The New York Times *(1904–14), his work also appeared in* Die Fliegende Blätter *(Munich),* Le Rire *(Paris), and* Black and White *(London). See Roland Burke Hennessy, "An Appreciation," in* Henry (Hy) Mayer, *Fantasies in* Ha! Ha! *(New York: Mayer Bros., 1900). There is also an amusing caricature of Mayer in C. De Fornare,* Mortals and Immortals *(New York: Hornet, 1911).*

V-57A *Paul A. Plaschke (1874–1951), "When Women Have Their Rights,"* Louisville Times, *Nov. 24, 1913. Like Hy Mayer, Plaschke was born in Germany. After thirty-six years of newspaper work in Louisville, he joined the* Chicago Herald and Examiner *in 1937. See* Editor & Publisher, *Jan. 23, 1937, p. 45, and* Who's Who in America, *Vol. XXII.*

V-58 *John F. Knott (1879–1963),*
"The two Adams: 'It was my rib,
Eve.'" Dallas Morning News, Aug.
29, 1920. See Werner Renberg,
"Old Man Texas Stands Up to
Uncle Sam," The Quill, Apr., 1951.

V-59 *Joseph Keppler, "A Cold*
Reception Everywhere," lithograph,
Puck, *July 3, 1889.*

V-60 *Rollin Kirby, "Now, then, all*
together: 'My Country 'tis of thee!'"
New York World, *Jan. 17, 1920.*
During Kirby's years on the New
York World *(1913–31) he won*
three Pulitzer Prizes; he remained
with the paper after a merger
turned it into the World Telegram
(1931–39), and then joined the
New York Post *(1939–42). When*
Prohibition was repealed in 1933,
Kirby officially buried his Mr.
Dry. "I was almost sorry to see
him go," said the cartoonist, "I was
almost getting fond of the old bum."
See Cecil Carnes, "Then He Found
A Shoe That Fit," The Quill, Apr.,
1939; H. R. Westwood, Modern
Caricaturists *(London: Loval*
Dickson, 1932), pp. 169–76; and
Rollin Kirby, Highlights, A Cartoon
History of the Nineteen Twenties
(New York: Farquhar Payson,
1931).

V-61 *"Temperance Advocate*
Preparing for the Operation of the
Liquor Law," wood engraving, The
Carpet Bag, *Aug. 21, 1852.*

V-62 *"Novel Effects of the*
Prohibition," wood engraving,
Yankee Notions, *June, 1855.*

V-62A *"Progress of Science Under*
the Maine Law," wood engraving,
Yankee Notions, *June, 1855.*

Progress of Science under the Maine Law.

Man (to licensed liquor seller.)—I WANT HALF A PINT OF BRANDY FOR
MECHANICAL PURPOSES.
Liquor Seller.—WHAT PURPOSE?
Man.—TO GET UP STEAM.

V-63 *H. T. Webster (1885–1952),* *"The Prohibitionist Finds a Horrid Old Dandelion on His Estate and Walks Half a Mile to Burn It in the Kitchen Stove,"* Brooklyn *Daily* Eagle, *July 8, 1920. Webster felt his career as a political cartoonist reached its height around 1908, when one of his drawings for the Chicago* Inter-Ocean *caused a man to laugh "so hard . . . while riding on the Elgin Electric that he had suffered a stroke and had to be carried off the train in a dangerous condition." Later, after turning to the comics, he earned a more lasting tribute by inventing a character, Caspar Milquetoast, whose surname would be defined in standard dictionaries. See John Monk Saunders, "This Cartoonist Gives Us a Look at Ourselves,"* American Magazine, *Sept., 1924, and Phil Calhoun, "Biographical Sketch," in* The Best of H. T. Webster *(New York: Simon & Schuster, 1953).*

V-63A *Daniel R. Fitzpatrick, "Samuel,"* St. Louis *Post-Dispatch, June 29, 1919.*

V-64 *Clive Weed (1884–1936), "The National Gesture,"* Judge, *June 12, 1926. See "Who's Who in* Judge," Judge, *Nov. 15, 1924, and "Cartoonists as They See Themselves,"* Literary Digest, *Jan. 20, 1934. Another interesting series, drawn by Carey Orr for the Chicago Tribune in 1929, was "The Truth About the Prohibition Killings," which basically were illustrated news stories such as one entitled, "The Killing of Ingmire," whose text read: "E. P. Ingmire, San Pedro, Cal., Business Man was killed and his wife was seriously injured, when the automobile in which they were riding was struck by a dry bureau car driven by Frank Farley, a Federal undercover dry agent. Farley and another dry agent, George Judson, both drunk, were joyriding with a woman and three other men, and had collided with another car just before killing Ingmire. Farley was indicted for first degree murder, but he succeeded in having the case transferred to the Federal Court, where he was permited to plead guilty to involuntary manslaughter. Judson, the other dry agent, was released."*

V-65 *Daniel R. Fitzpatrick, "One Person Out of Every Ten," St. Louis* Post-Dispatch, *Jan. 16, 1938.*

V-66 *Clarence D. Batchelor (b. 1888), "Yes, You Remembered Me," New York* Sunday News, *Oct. 11, 1936.*

V-67 *Herbert Johnson (1878–1946), "Nonsense! If it gets too deep, you can easily pull me out!"* Saturday Evening Post, *Sept. 28, 1935. Copyright 1935 Curtis Publishing Company. Courtesy Mrs. Kathrine Johnson Evans and Mrs. Herberta J. Muth.*

V-67A *Another example of an anti-New Deal cartoon. Carey Orr (1890–1967), "The Trojan Horse at Our Gate," Chicago* Tribune, *Sept. 17, 1935. Orr retired in 1963 after forty-six years with the Tribune. He won a Pulitzer Prize in 1961 and taught a generation of cartoonists at the Chicago Academy of Fine Arts.*

V-68 *Jay N. Darling, "Halloween 1936," New York* Herald Tribune, *Oct. 31, 1936. His last name was Darling, but he signed his cartoons "Ding." "I want to avoid appearing sentimental," he explained in 1903 when he was drawing for his hometown paper in Sioux City, Iowa. By 1911 Darling had been lured to New York, but he longed for Iowa. So he worked out an arrangement by which he could live in Des Moines, draw for the* Register *of that city, and have his cartoons syndicated nationally by the New York* Tribune *(later the Herald Tribune). His cartoons, which looked as if they were done with pen but were actually drawn on a very large scale with a brush, earned him two Pulitzer Prizes. He retired in 1949, after a career of almost a half century and 17,000 cartoons.*

217

'Bye Now — It's Been Wonderful Knowing You

V-68A *Ding drew this farewell in 1958 and gave it to his secretary with instructions to keep it hidden until his death. It appeared in the* New York *Herald-Tribune on Feb. 13, 1962. Besides depicting his most famous cartoon ("The Long, Long Trail," upper left), it also reflects his love of ducks (he was once Chief of the U.S. Biological Survey) and the Iowa farmer. His style lives on in the work of his disciple, Dan Dowling, who, after the demise of the New York World Journal Tribune, became cartoonist for the Kansas City Star. See Henry Schott, "J. N. Ding, Who Puts a Smile in Economics,"* Nation's Business, *May, 1925; Beverly Smith, "A Cartoonist Shows a State How to Enjoy Life,"* American Magazine, *Apr., 1933; Tom Mahoney, "How to Be a Cartoonist,"* Saturday Evening Post, *Oct. 19, 1940; and J. N. Darling,* Ding's Half Century *(New York: Duell, Sloan & Pierce, 1962).*

13. See Dale Kramer, *Ross and the New Yorker* (Garden City, N.Y.: Doubleday, 1951), and James Thurber, *The Years with Ross* (Boston: Little, Brown, 1959).

V-69 *William Galbraith Crawford (b. 1894), "And if Roosevelt is not reelected, perhaps even a villa in Newport, my dearest sweet,"* The New Yorker, *Mar. 28, 1936. Since 1939, "Galbraith" has been doing a panel called "Side Glances" for NEA. See Martin Sheridan,* Comics and their Creators *(Hale, Cushman & Flint, 1942), p. 267.*

V-70 *Robert Day (b. 1900), "For gosh sakes, here comes Mrs. Roosevelt!"* The New Yorker, *June 3, 1933.*

V-71 *Ross Lewis (b. 1902), "The Sphinx Speaks, But Says Nothing,"* Milwaukee Journal, *Nov. 22, 1939. Lewis, whose style was influenced by his teacher, Boardman Robinson, served as cartoonist for the* Milwaukee Journal *from 1932 until 1967. He won the Pulitzer Prize in 1935.*

V-72 *Tom Little (b. 1898), "My Little Dog Fala Is Furious!"* Nashville Tennessean, *Sept. 26, 1944. Courtesy Tennessee State Library and Archives, Nashville. Little was the city editor of the* Tennessean *until he succumbed to the urge to draw and became his paper's poltical cartoonist in 1934. He won the Pulitzer Prize in 1957.*

14. Gerald Johnson, *op. cit.,* p. 167; also see Herbert Block, *The Herblock Book* (Boston: Beacon, 1952), pp. 22–4.

V-73 *Edwin Marcus, "One Dim Out We Can't Have,"* The New York Times, *Dec. 1, 1946, pen and ink drawing. Before World War I, Marcus' cartoons ran a full page.*

He succeeded Hy Mayer, thus becoming the second and last political cartoonist of The New York Times; *the paper did not replace him when he retired after fifty years' service in 1958.*

V-74 *Lute Pease (1869–1963), "How Does He Do It?"* Newark Evening News, *Apr. 13, 1948, pen and ink drawing. Lute Pease joined the Newark* Evening News *in 1914 and was still with that paper in 1949 when, five weeks after his eightieth birthday, he won the Pulitzer Prize. His prize-winning cartoon was about John L. Lewis, who also figured in the 1944 Pulitzer Prize winner by Clifford K. Berryman.*

V-75 *Harold M. Talburt (1895–1966), "Warning to Samson! An Avalanche of Anti-labor Legislation,"* Washington Daily News, *May 7, 1943, pencil drawing. For other cartoons that depict Lewis as Samson see Fred O. Seibel of the* Richmond Times-Dispatch, *reprinted in* The New York Times, *Jan. 5, 1958, and Charles Werner of the* Chicago Sun, *reprinted in* The Quill, *Sept.-Oct., 1944, p. 12. Talburt, the chief editorial cartoonist for the Scripps-Howard newspapers from 1922 until 1963, never used pen or brush but did his drawings in pencil. He won the Pulitzer Prize in 1933.*

V-76 *Charles Werner (b. 1909), "Old Faithful!"* Indianapolis Star, *Aug. 12, 1952. Pencil drawing. Werner, then of the* Daily Oklahoman *(Oklahoma City), won the Pulitzer Prize in 1939 during his first year as a full-time cartoonist. He was the youngest man so honored up to that time. See* " 'Cartoon Must Criticize to Be Good'—Werner," *Editor & Publisher, Apr. 20, 1946.*

V-77 *Clarence D. Batchelor, "Come on in. I'll treat you right. I*

used to know your daddy," New York Daily News, *Apr. 25, 1936. See Ann Lord, "Behind the Batchelor Byline,"* The Quill, *Dec., 1939.*

V-78 *Daniel R. Fitzpatrick, "Swastika over Germany,"* St. Louis Post-Dispatch, *Sept. 17, 1935. Fitzpatrick spent forty-five years with the* Post-Dispatch, *retiring in 1958. For appreciations of the artist, who ranks among the top half-dozen cartoonists the United States has produced, see Thomas B. Sherman, "Profile of a Cartoonist," in D. R. Fitzpatrick,* As I Saw It *(New York: Simon & Schuster, 1953), and Irving Dilliard, "Editor to Cartoonist,"* The Quill, *Oct., 1951.*

V-79 *Daniel R. Fitzpatrick, "Next!"* St. Louis Post-Dispatch, *Aug. 24, 1939.*

V-80 *Vaughn Shoemaker (b. 1902), "Take me to Czechoslovakia, driver,"* Chicago Daily News, *Sept. 8, 1938. Shoemaker was with the* Daily News *from 1922 until 1951, at which time he joined the New York Herald Tribune Syndicate. In 1962 he became the chief cartoonist of the Chicago's American. See George A. Brandenburg, "Vaughn Shoemaker Tells His Cartooning Creed,"* Editor & Publisher, *Aug. 6, 1938, and William A. Rutledge, III, "The Life Guard and the Lady,"* The Quill, *Sept. 1938.*

V-81 *Vaughn Shoemaker, "Path of Appeasement,"* Chicago Daily News, *Nov. 28, 1940.*

V-82 *Herbert L. Block, "I Have Here in my Hand,"* Washington Post, *May 7, 1954. See Herbert L. Block,* The Herblock Book; *op. cit.;* Herblock's Here and Now *(New York: Simon & Schuster, 1955);* Herblock's Special for Today *(New*

York: Simon & Schuster, 1958);
Straight Herblock (New York:
Simon & Schuster, 1964).

15. See Philip Potter, "Political
Pitchman, Richard M. Nixon," in
Eric Sevareid, ed., *Candidates
1960* (New York: Basic Books,
1959), p. 81, and John D. Weaver,
"Drawing Blood," *Holiday,* Aug.,
1965, p. 72. Nixon had another
personal experience with cartooning
in 1955 when a San Francisco art
exhibit included a caricature of the
Vice President as a black-masked
hoodlum. The head of the city art
commission ordered the lithograph,
entitled "Dick McSmear," removed
from the show, but Nixon wired
that "one of the most sacred
precepts of our Anglo-American
legal heritage is the right of
individuals to criticize public
officials," See James Keogh, *This Is
Nixon* (New York: Putnam's, 1956),
pp. 72, 73.

V-83   *Herbert L. Block, "Here He
Comes Now," Washington Post,
Oct. 29, 1954. "If he lives to be a
hundred," said a friend of Nixon's
to Theodore H. White, Nixon will
"never forget that Herblock cartoon
of the welcoming committee, and
him climbing out of the sewer to
greet it . . ." See Theodore H.
White,* The Making of the President
1960 *(New York: Atheneum, 1961),
p. 266.*

V-84   *Edmund Duffy (1899–1962),
"Put it on again!" Baltimore Sun,
Jan. 23, 1928. See Dick Spencer, III,
Pulitzer Prize Cartoons (Ames:
Iowa State College Press, 1951),
pp. 42–5, 54–7.*

V-85   *Reginald Marsh
(1898–1954), "This is her first
lynching," The New Yorker, Sept. 8,
1934. See Norman Sasowsky,
Reginald Marsh (New York:
Praeger, 1956).*

V-85A   *Pierre Bellocq (Peb)
(b. 1926), "Southern Hospitality,"
Philadelphia* Inquirer, *May 8, 1963.*

V-85B   *Thomas F. Flannery
(b. 1919), "Stars Fell on Alabama,"
Baltimore* Evening Sun, *May 9,
1963.*

V-86   Bill Mauldin, "See you in church," Chicago Sun-Times, Sept. 16, 1962.

V-87   Bill Mauldin, "I've decided I want my seat back," Chicago Sun-Times, Sept. 6, 1963. See Bill Mauldin, Up Front (New York: Henry Holt, 1945); A Sort of Saga (New York: Sloane, 1949); What's Got Your Back Up? (New York: Harper & Row, 1965), "A Cartoonist Goes Campaigning," Collier's, Sept. 28, 1956. See also Time cover story, July 21, 1961.

V-88   Jules Feiffer (b. 1929), "Pardon me, why are you following me?" Hall Syndicate, Sept. 8, 1963. See Jules Feiffer, Boy, Girl, Boy, Girl (New York: Random House, 1961); Hold Me! (New York: Random House, 1962); Feiffer on Civil Rights (New York: Anti-Defamation League of B'nai B'rith, 1966); The Great Comic Book Heroes (New York: Dial, 1965); and Print, Jan.-Feb., 1966.

V-89   John Fischetti (b. 1916), "A new hot line from the White House to Capitol Hill," New York Herald Tribune, Dec. 12, 1963. Courtesy Publishers-Hall Syndicate. Pen and ink drawing.

V-90   Frank Interlandi (b. 1924), "There's no room in the shelter," copyright 1961, Los Angeles Times.

V-91   Edmund S. Valtman (b. 1914), "We will fight to the last Vietnamese any U.S. attempt for a negotiated peace!" Hartford Times, Sept. 14, 1965.

V-92   Bill Sanders (b. 1930), "Courage, lad, you'll be good as new in no time!" Milwaukee Journal, Oct. 20, 1967.

V-93   Ray Orsin (b. 1928), "Besides, think of all those commodities falling off the edge of the earth," Cleveland Plain Dealer, Oct. 18, 1967.

V-94   Tom Darcy (b. 1932), "I'll guard the fort, Gene—you go down and see what they want," Philadelphia Bulletin, Jan. 21, 1968.

V-95   Draper Hill (b. 1935), "That Personal Touch," Worcester Telegram, March 15, 1966. See Florence R. Niles, "Cartoons by Hill at Casdin Gallery," Worcester Evening Gazette, Mar. 22, 1966, p. 32; Julian F. Grow, "A Cartoon is Born—The Mind Behind the Man Behind the Pen," Worcester Sunday Telegram, Mar. 10, 1968.

V-96   Hugh Haynie (b. 1927), "If you won't play my way, I'll take my ball and go home," Louisville Courier-Journal, July 7, 1965. See "Quick on the Draw," Newsweek, Mar. 19, 1962, pp. 112–13.

V-97   Jerry Robinson (b. 1922), "What is a Limited War?" Chicago Tribune–New York News Syndicate, May 7, 1966.

V-98   David Levine (b. 1926), untitled, New York Review of Books, May 12, 1966. Copyright 1966 The New York Book Review. See David Levine, The Man From M.A.L.I.C.E. (New York: Dutton, 1966), and Hilton Kramer, "Hard to Dissect Beloved Rembrandt," The New York Times, December 17, 1966, p. 29.

V-99   Wayne Stayskal (b. 1931), "Cupid," Chicago's American, May 31, 1967.

V-100   Paul Szep, "A Senator Fulbright to see you, Sire. Seems he can't reconcile himself to your infallibility," Boston Globe, Aug. 18, 1967. See Paul Szep, In Search of Sacred Cows (Boston: Boston Globe, 1968).

V-101   Paul Conrad (b. 1924), "Flag Razing in Central Park," Los Angeles Times, Apr. 18, 1967.

V-102   Paul Conrad, "Ky's Cabinet," Los Angeles Times, Oct. 24, 1966. See "One of the Few," Time, June 13, 1960, pp. 52–3.

V-103   Patrick B. Oliphant (b. 1936), "I'll tell you this much, you'd never get me up in one of them things!" Denver Post, May 4, 1967. See "Down Under to Denver," Time, Sept. 18, 1964, pp. 82–3, and "O is for Oliphant," The Congressional Record, May 25, 1967, p. A2647.

V-104   Patrick B. Oliphant, untitled, Denver Post, May 30, 1967.

16. "The Limits of Caricature," The Nation, July 19, 1866, p. 55.

17. Quoted in W. B. Blake, "The American Cartoon," The Independent, Jan. 23, 1913, p. 216.

18. C. D. Batchelor, "Daily News Artist Deplores Standardization," Art News, Oct., 1954.

19. Frederick Richardson, "The Education of the Newspaper Artist," The American Cartoonist, Nov., 1903.

Acknowledgments

Our first acknowledged debt must be to Don Hesse, cartoonist for the St. Louis *Globe-Democrat,* from whom we have borrowed the phrase *The Ungentlemanly Art,* a title that originally graced his article in *The Quill,* December, 1959.

We are especially grateful to two learned gentlemen who read our manuscript and filled its margins with many useful comments: Alan Fern, Assistant Chief, Prints and Photographs Division, Library of Congress; and Draper Hill, author of the classic two-volume study of James Gillray.

All plates, unless otherwise indicated in the footnotes, came from material in the Library of Congress, Washington, D.C., and were photographed by the excellent staff of the Library's Photoduplication Service.

Much logistical support for this project has been graciously given at the Institute of Politics, John F. Kennedy School of Government, Harvard University, Cambridge, Massachusetts, in which Stephen Hess was a Fellow during the final months of the book's preparation. Our deepest thanks go to Professor Richard E. Neustadt, the Institute's Director; Mrs. Mary Lanigan, administrative assistant; and Miss Nancy Lyons and Mrs. Nicole MacInnes, secretaries.

We are grateful to our friends at Macmillan: Peter V. Ritner, Editor-in-Chief; Abe Lerner, Director of Design and Production; and Robert Myer, Production Editor. We are further indebted to the publisher for choosing the talented and always patient Herbert M. Rosenthal as the designer.

Among the many institutions and organizations whose cooperation was sought and cheerfully given were: Alabama Department of Archives and History, Montgomery; American Antiquarian Society, Worcester, Massachusetts; Archives of American Art, Detroit; Baltimore *Evening Sun;* Boston Athenaeum; Boston Public Library; Chicago Tribune–New York News Syndicate; Copy Company, Seattle; The Curtis Publishing Company, New York; District of Columbia Public Library; Fogg Museum of Fine Arts, Harvard University; The Historical Society of Pennsylvania, Philadelphia; Houghton Library, Harvard University; Henry E. Huntington Library and Art Gallery, San Marino, California; Edwin B. Luce Company, Worcester; The Mariners Museum, Newport News, Virginia; The Memorial Library, University of Wisconsin, Madison; Metropolitan Museum of Art, New York; Museum of Fine Arts, Boston; Nashville *Tennessean;* New England Deposit Library, Boston; New-York Historical Society, New York; New York City Public Library; *The New Yorker;* Newspaper Enterprises Association, Cleveland; The Philadelphia *Inquirer;* Publishers– Hall Syndicate, New York; St. Louis, Missouri, Public Library; Seattle, Washington, Public Library; State Historical Society of Wisconsin, Madison; Tennessee State Library and Archives, Nashville; United Press International; University of Missouri, Columbia; University of Texas Library, Austin; and Widener Library, Harvard University.

Many individuals have given generously of their time and knowledge. We thank Peggy Bacon, Cape Porpoise, Maine; Rex Barley, Los Angeles; Carey S. Bliss, San Marino, California; Herbert L. Block, Washington, D.C.; Glenn H. Borders, Washington, D.C.; Jacob Burck, Chicago; B. D. Cain, Nashville; Robert C. Couper, San Jose, California; Thomas Darcy, Philadelphia; Robert Eckhardt, Houston; Gerald A. Elliott, Grand Rapids, Michigan; Ira Emerich, New York; Mrs. Katherine Johnson Evans, Newtown, Pennsylvania; Jules Feiffer, New York; Mrs. Caroline Fisher, Cambridge; John Fischetti, Chicago; D. R. Fitzpatrick, St. Louis; J. J. Fletcher, New York; James R. Galbraith, Washington, D.C.; Jack Gamble, Cleveland; Gerald Gardner, Hollywood, California; Mrs. Wendy O. Goodall, Boston; Harold F. Grumhaus, Chicago; Miss Nancy Hall, New York; Miss Jean I. Hare, Baltimore; Miss Phoebe Harris, Seattle; Hugh Haynie, Louisville; Miss Louise Henning, Madison, Wisconsin; Sinclair H. Hitchings, Boston; Miss Judith A. Hoffberg, Philadelphia; Milo B. Howard, Montgomery, Alabama; Miss Barbara Hufham, New York; Gerald W. Johnson, Baltimore; Daniel Jones, New York; Herbert A. Kenny, Boston; John D. Kilbourne, Philadelphia; William Holt Kling, Washington; Mrs. Philip B. Kunhardt, New York; David Levine, New York; John Lochhead, Newport News, Virginia; Marcus A. McCorison, Worcester, Massachusetts; Mrs. John T. McCutcheon, Lake Forest, Illinois; James Marshall, Washington; Mrs. Louise Marshall, Worcester, Massachusetts; Bill Mauldin, Chicago; Miss Bea Moore, New York; Miss Hazel Murdock, Columbia, Missouri; Mrs. Herberta J. Muth, Newtown, Pennsylvania; Patrick Oliphant, Denver; Ray Osrin, Cleveland; Theodore Peruche, New York; Henry Raduta, New York; Mrs. Ruth C. Rogin, New York; Jerry Robinson, New York; Claire Rosenstein, New York; Bill Sanders, Milwaukee; Mrs. Martha Scharff, St. Louis; H. H. Schnabel, Jr., Boston; Harry Schwartz, Washington; Raymond Shapiro, New York; Vaughn Shoemaker, Chicago; Wayne Stayskal, Chicago; Paul Szep, Boston; Paul Theis, Washington; Edmund S. Valtman, Hartford, Connecticut; Charles Werner, Indianapolis; Harold J. Weigand, Philadelphia; and Art Wood, Washington.

The Ungentlemanly Art probably should have been subtitled "Why Didn't You Use the One About . . ." For cartoon buffs are an opinionated lot. We could plead space limitations; but we would rather plead prejudice—indeed, we feel ourselves as entitled to our cherished biases as any other reader who chuckles or groans over the morning's Herblock, Mauldin, Conrad or Oliphant. Thus this volume stands as a monument to our fallibility.

Finally, we should like to recall *The Ungentlemanly Art*'s subtitle: "A History of American Political Cartoons." We never meant this book to be a political history of America in cartoons. By generally choosing to tell our story in order of occurrence we hope that some of the broad sweep of the nation's past is evident. Yet our purpose was not to chronicle how cartoonists have treated thirty-six Presidents or eight wars. While we are sorry if a favorite statesman is missing from these pages, we offer no apology.

STEPHEN HESS

MILTON KAPLAN

May 14, 1968

Bibliography

Abbott, Lyman, "Cartoons and Caricatures in War Time," *The Outlook,* Nov. 8, 1916.

American Caricature Pertaining to the Civil War. New York: Brentano's, 1918.

Arkell, W. J., *Old Friends and Some Acquaintances.* Los Angeles: privately printed, 1927.

"The Art of Political Cartoons," *The Living Age,* Apr. 24, 1920.

"The Artist as Social Critic," *Print,* Jan.–Feb., 1966.

Attwood, Francis G., *Attwood's Pictures. An Artist's History of the Last Ten Years of the Nineteenth Century.* New York: Life Publishing, 1900.

Bacon, Peggy, *Off With Their Heads!* New York: McBride, 1934.

Baer, John M., "Cartoons and Success," *Pep,* Aug., 1918.

Bartholomew, Charles L., and others, *Applied Cartooning.* Minneapolis: Federal School of Applied Cartooning, 1920.

——, *Bart's Cartoons for 1902 from the Minneapolis Journal.* Minneapolis: Journal Printing Co., 1903.

——, *Cartoons of the Spanish-American War by Bart.* Minneapolis: Journal, 1899.

Bartow, Edith Merwin, *News and These United States.* New York: Funk & Wagnalls, 1952.

Batchelor, Clarence D., "Daily News Artist Deplores Standardization," *Art News,* Oct., 1954.

——, *Truman Scrapbook.* Deep River, Conn.: Kelsey Hill Publishing, 1951.

Bayley, Frank W., and Charles E. Goodspeed, eds., *A History of the Rise and Progress of the Arts of Design in the United States.* New York: Goodspeed, 1918.

Beard, Frank, "Caricature," *The Manhattan,* Feb., 1884.

——, *Fifty Great Cartoons.* Chicago: Ram's Horn, 1899.

Beardsley, William A., *An Old New Haven Engraver and His Work: Amos Doolittle.* Photostat in Library of Congress, 1910.

Becker, Stephen, *Comic Art in America.* New York: Simon & Schuster, 1959.

Berry, Jim. *Berry's World.* New York: Four Winds, 1967.

Berryman, Clifford K., *Berryman Cartoons.* Washington: Saks & Co., 1900.

——, *Berryman's Cartoons of the 58th House.* Washington: C. K. Berryman, 1903.

——, *Development of the Cartoon.* Columbia, Mo.: University of Missouri Bulletin, 1926.

Birchman, Willis, *Faces & Facts By and About 26 Contemporary Artists.* Privately printed, 1937.

Bishop, Joseph Bucklin, "Early Political Caricature in America," *Century Magazine,* June, 1892.

——, *Our Political Drama.* New York: Scott–Thaw, 1904.

Blake, W. B., "The American Cartoon," *The Independent,* Jan. 23, 1913.

Block, Herbert L., *The Herblock Book.* Boston: Beacon Press, 1952.

——, *Herblock's Here and Now.* New York: Simon & Schuster, 1955.

——, *Herblock's Special for Today.* New York: Simon & Schuster, 1958.

——, *Straight Herblock.* New York: Simon & Schuster, 1964.

Blunt, Abbot, "Roland C. [Doc] Bowman," *The American Cartoonist,* Aug., 1903.

Bowman, Rowland Claude, *The Tribune Cartoon Book for 1901.* Minneapolis: Tribune Printing, 1901.

——, *The Tribune Cartoon Book for 1902.* Minneapolis: Tribune Printing, 1902.

Bradley, Luther D., *Cartoons by Bradley.* Chicago: Rand McNally, 1917.

Brandenburg, George A., "Vaughn Shoemaker Tells His Cartooning Creed," *Editor & Publisher,* Aug. 6, 1938.

Brewerton, A. W., *Drawing for Newspapers.* Atlanta: American Publishing, 1910.

Brigham, Clarence S., *Paul Revere's Engravings.* Worcester, Mass.: American Antiquarian Society, 1954.

Burck, Jacob, "Cartooning is Like This," *The Masthead,* winter, 1950.

——, *Our 34th President.* Chicago: Chicago Sun-Times, 1953.

Butterfield, Roger, *The American Past.* New York: Simon & Schuster, 1947.

Byrnes, Gene, *The Complete Guide to Cartooning.* New York: Grosset & Dunlap, 1950.

The Campaign of '48 in Star Cartoons. Washington: Evening Star, 1948.

The Campaign of '52 in Star Cartoons. Washington: Evening Star, 1952.

The Campaign of '56 in Star Cartoons. Washington: Evening Star, 1956.

"Caricature in America," *All The Year Round,* Sept. 28, 1878.

Carnes, Cecil, "Then He Found a Shoe That Fit [Rollin Kirby]," *The Quill,* Apr., 1939.

Cartoons of the War of 1898 with Spain. Chicago: Belford, Middlebrook, 1898.

Caruso, Enrico, *The New Book of Caricature by Enrico Caruso.* New York: La Follia di New York, 1965.

Catalogue of the Salon of American Humorists, A Political and Social Pageant from the Revolution to the Present Day. New York: College Art Association, 1933.

Cesare, Oscar, *One Hundred Cartoons.* Boston: Small, Maynard, 1916.

Chapin, Will E., *Cartoons of Will E. Chapin.* Los Angeles: Times–Mirror, 1899.

Chase, John, *Today's Cartoon.* New Orleans: Hauser Press, 1962.

Clubb, John Scott, *Cartoons.* Rochester, N.Y.: Herald, 1901.

Conningham, F. A., *Currier & Ives.* Cleveland & New York: World, 1950.

Contemporary Cartoons, An Exhibition of Original Drawings. San Marino, Cal.: Huntington Library, 1937.

Craven, Thomas, ed., *Cartoon Cavalcade.* New York: Simon & Schuster, 1943.

Croker, Richard, *Poltical Cartoons Gathered by Their Target.* New York: Mitchell, n.d.

Crosby, Percy, *Always Belittlin'.* McLean, Va.: Percy Crosby, 1933.

Crouse, Russel, *Mr. Currier and Mr. Ives.* Garden City, N.Y.: Doubleday, Doran, 1930.

Cuff, Roger Penn, "The American Editorial Cartoon—A Critical Historical Sketch," *The Journal of Educational Sociology,* Oct., 1945.

Dahl, Francis, *Dahl's Boston*. Boston: Little, Brown, 1946.

——, *What! More Dahl?* Boston: Hale, 1944.

Darling, Jay N., *As Ding Saw Hoover*. Ames, Iowa: Iowa State College Press, 1954.

——, *Cartoons from the Files of The Register & Leader*. Des Moines: Register & Leader, 1908.

——, *Ding's Half Century*. New York: Duell, Sloan & Pearce, 1962.

——, *The Education of Alonzo Applegate and Other Cartoons*. Des Moines: Register & Leader, 1910.

——, *Midwest Farming as Portrayed by a Selection from Ding's Cartoons*. Des Moines, Iowa: Pioneer Hi-Bred Corn Co., 1960.

Darvas, Lou, *You Can Draw Cartoons*. Garden City, N.Y.: Doubleday, 1960.

Davenport, Homer, *Cartoons*. New York: De Witt, 1898.

——, *The Dollar or the Man?* Boston: Small, Maynard, 1900.

——, "The Gentle Art of Making the Wicked Squirm," New York *Journal*, Apr. 16, 1899.

——, "The Personal Narrative of Homer Davenport," *The Pacific Monthly*, Nov. and Dec., 1905.

——, *My Quest of the Arab Horse*. New York: Dodge, 1909.

De Fornaro, C., *Mortals and Immortals*. New York: Hornet, 1911.

Dilliard, Irving, "Indiana's Three Well Known Cartoonists," *The Quill*, Nov., 1959.

Dobbins, Jim, *Dobbins' History of the New Frontier*. Boston: Humphries, 1964.

Donahey, James H., *Donahey's Cartoons*. Cleveland: Vinson & Korner, 1900.

Downey, Fairfax, *Portrait of an Era as Drawn by C. D. Gibson*. New York: Scribner's, 1936.

Drepperd, Carl., *Early American Prints*. New York & London: Century, 1930.

Eastman, Joel W., *The Maine Thing, Some of My Best Friends are Republicans*. Freeport, Me.: Bond Wheelwright, 1964.

Feiffer, Jules, *Feiffer on Civil Rights*. New York: Anti-Defamation League of B'nai B'rith, 1966.

——, *The Great Comic Book Heroes*. New York: Dial, 1965.

——, *Hold Me!* New York: Random House, 1962.

Fitzpatrick, Daniel R., *As I Saw It*. New York: Simon & Schuster, 1953.

——, "Cartoonist to Editor," *The Quill*, Oct., 1951.

——, "Two Blocks in One," *The New Republic*, Oct., 13, 1952.

Flagg, James Montgomery, *Roses and Buckshot*. New York: Putnam's, 1946.

Flower, B. O., "Dan. Beard: The Man and His Art," *The Arena*, July, 1904.

——, "DeMar: A Cartoonist of Contemporaneous History," *The Arena*, Dec., 1905.

——, "Floyd Campbell: A Knight of Municipal Honor," *The Arena*, Oct., 1905.

——, "Frederick Opper: A Cartoonist of Democracy," *The Arena,* June, 1905.

——, "Garnet Warren: Cartoonist," *The Arena,* Feb., 1905.

——, "G. R. Spencer: A Cartoonist of Progressive Democracy and Aggressive Honesty," *The Arena,* Oct., 1906.

——, "Homer Davenport: A Cartoonist Dominated by Moral Ideals," *The Arena,* July , 1905.

——, "J. Campbell Cory: Cartoonist," *The Arena,* Jan., 1906.

——, "J. Sidney Craiger: An Iowa Cartoonist," *The Arena,* Mar., 1906.

——, "Roy D. Handy: One of the Youngest of our Newspaper Cartoonists," *The Arena,* Feb., 1906.

——, "Ryan Walker: A Cartoonist of Social Protest," *The Arena,* Apr., 1905.

——, "W. A. Rogers: The Cartoonist of Civic Integrity," *The Arena,* Apr., 1906.

——, "W. Gordon Nye: A Cartoonist of Jeffersonian Democracy," *The Arena,* Aug., 1906.

Forbes, Esther, *Paul Revere and the World He Lived In.* Boston: Houghton Mifflin, 1942.

Ford, James L., *Forty-Odd Years in the Literary Shop.* New York: Dutton, 1921.

Fullerton, Hugh S., "Answering the Query: Are Cartoonists Human?" *Collier's,* Nov. 8, 1924.

Garrison, Lloyd McK., "The Work of a Great Cartoonist [Francis Gilbert Attwood]," *The Cosmopolitan,* Sept., 1900.

Gibson, Charles Dana, "Cartoons and Cartoonists," *The Mentor,* Oct., 1923.

Goldberg, Rube, "Comics, New Style and Old," *The Saturday Evening Post,* Dec. 15, 1928.

——, "It Happened to a Rube," *The Saturday Evening Post,* Nov. 10, 1928.

——, "My Answer to the Question: How Did You Put It Over? The Story of How I Became a Cartoonist," *The American Magazine,* Mar., 1922.

Goodrich, Lloyd, *John Sloan,* New York: Macmillan, 1952.

Gropper, William, *Gropper.* New York: ACA Gallery Publications, 1938.

——, *Gropper, Twelve Etchings with a Foreward by Alan Fern.* New York 1965.

Gros, Raymond, *T. R. in Cartoon,* Akron: Saalfield, 1910.

Gutman, Walter, "An American Phenomenon [Thomas Nast]," *Creative Art,* July–Dec., 1929.

Halsey, R. T. H., "English Sympathy With Boston During the American Revolution," *Old-Time New England,* Apr.–June, 1956

Hammer, Mrs. D. Harry, "Cartoons of Uncle Sam," *Cartoons Magazine,* July, 1913.

——, "The Translators of Uncle Sam," *Cartoons Magazine,* June, 1913.

Hancock, La Touche, "American Caricature and Comic Art," *The Bookman,* Oct. and Nov.,1902.

Harding, Nelson, *The Political Campaign of 1912 in Cartoons*. Brooklyn, N.Y.: Daily Eagle, 1912.

Harley, Robert A., "What Cartoonists Say About Their Work," *The Ohio Newspaper,* Dec., 1931.

Harwell, Richard Barksdale, "Confederate Anti-Lincoln Literature," *Lincoln Herald,* fall, 1951.

Heaton, Harold R., *"Events of the Week" Reprinted from the Chicago Tribune*. Chicago: Shepard, 1894.

Hecht, George, "How the Cartoonist Can Help Win the War," *Cartoons Magazine,* Feb., 1918.

———, *The War in Cartoons*. New York: Dutton, 1919.

Heimer, Mel, *Famous Artists and Writers of King Features Syndicate*. New York: King Features, 1946.

Heintzelman, Arthur W., *The Watercolor Drawings of Thomas Rowlandson*. New York: Watson–Guptill, 1947.

Herford, Oliver, *Confessions of a Caricaturist*. New York: Scribner's, 1917.

Hesse, Don, "The Ungentlemanly Art," *The Quill,* Dec., 1959.

Hill, Draper, *Fashionable Contrasts, Caricatures by James Gillray*. London: Phaidon, 1966.

———, *Mr. Gillray, The Caricaturist*. London: Phaidon, 1965.

———, *"What Fools These Mortals Be!" A Study of the Work of Joseph Keppler—Founder of Puck*. Unpublished A.B. thesis, Harvard College, 1957.

"Historical Campaign Caricatures," *The World's Work,* Nov., 1900.

Hoffman, Frederick J., Charles Allen, and Carolyn F. Ulrich, *The Little Magazine, A History and a Bibliography*. Princeton: Princeton University Press, 1946.

Hofmann, Werner, *Caricature from Leonardo to Picasso*. New York: Crown, 1957.

"Homer Davenport—Cartoonist," *Review of Reviews,* June, 1912.

Johnson, Gerald W., *The Lines Are Drawn*. Philadelphia & New York: Lippincott, 1958.

Johnson, Herbert, *Cartoons by Herbert Johnson*. Philadelphia: Lippincott, 1936.

———, "Why Cartoon—and How," *The Saturday Evening Post,* July 14, 1928.

Keidel, George C., *Dr. Adalbert J. Volck, Caricaturist, and His Family, Personal Reminiscences*. Typewritten manuscript, Library of Congress, n.d.

Keller, Morton, *The Art and Politics of Thomas Nast*. New York: Oxford University Press, 1968.

Kelly, Walt, *The Ever-Lovin' Blue-Eyed Years with Pogo*. New York: Simon & Schuster, 1959.

———, "Pogo Looks at the Abominable Snowman," *Saturday Review,* Aug. 30, 1958.

Kirby, Rollin, *Highlights, A Cartoon History of the Nineteen Twenties.* New York: Payson, 1931.

——, "My Creed as a Cartoonist," *Pep,* Dec., 1918.

Knaufft, Ernest, "Thomas Nast," *Review of Reviews,* Jan., 1903.

Kramer, Dale, *Ross and The New Yorker.* Garden City, N.Y.: Doubleday, 1951.

Lariar, Lawrence, *Careers in Cartooning.* New York: Dodd, Mead, 1949.

Lee, James Melvin, "Lincoln as Vanity Fair Saw Him," *Cartoons Magazine,* Feb., 1916.

——, "Punchinello and Its Cartoons," *Cartoons Magazine,* Aug., 1916.

——, "Wordless Journalism," *Cartoons Magazine,* April, May, and June, 1915.

Levine, David, *The Man from M.A.L.I.C.E.* New York: Dutton, 1966.

"The Limits of Caricature," *The Nation,* July 19, 1866.

Long, Scott, "The Cartoon Is a Weapon," *The Masthead,* fall, 1961.

——, "The Political Cartoon: Journalism's Strongest Weapon," *The Quill,* Nov., 1962.

Lorant, Stefan, *The Presidency.* New York: Macmillan, 1953.

Lord, Ann, "Behind the Batchelor Byline," *The Quill,* Dec., 1939.

Lovey, Alan L., *Cartoons by Lovey.* Salt Lake City: Lovey Fund, 1907.

Lyons, L. M., "The Humor of Herblock," *Nieman Reports,* Jan., 1953.

McCutcheon, John T., *Cartoons by McCutcheon.* Chicago: McClurg, 1903.

——, *The Cartoons That Made Prince Henry Famous.* Chicago: Record-Herald, 1902.

——, *Drawn from Memory.* Indianapolis & New York: Bobbs-Merrill, 1950.

——, *The Mysterious Stranger and Other Cartoons:* New York: McClure, Phillips, 1905.

——, *T. R. in Cartoons.* Chicago: McClurg, 1903.

McDougall, Walt, *This is the Life!* New York: Knopf, 1926.

Mahoney, Tom, "How to Be a Cartoonist," *The Saturday Evening Post,* Oct. 19, 1940.

Mannering, Mitchell, "Historical Cartoons in American Politics," *National Magazine,* Nov., 1900.

"A Master Cartoonist [Charles G. Bush]," *The World's Work,* Feb., 1901.

Matthews, Albert, *Brother Jonathan.* Cambridge, Mass.: Wilson, 1902.

——, *Uncle Sam.* Worcester, Mass.: Davis Press, 1908.

Matthews, J. Brander, "The Comic Periodical Literature of the United States," *The American Bibliopolist,* Aug., 1875.

Mauldin, Bill, *I've Decided I Want My Seat Back.* New York: Harper & Row, 1965.

——, *A Sort of a Saga.* New York: Sloane, 1949.

——, *Up Front.* New York: Holt, 1945.

——, *What's Got Your Back Up?* New York: Harper, 1961.

Maurice, Arthur Bartlett, ed., "Cartoons That Have Swayed History," *The Mentor,* July, 1930.

——, *How They Draw Prohibition.* New York: The Association Against the Prohibition Amendment, 1930.

——, "Thomas Nast and His Cartoons," *The Bookman,* Mar., 1902.

Maurice, Arthur Bartlett, and Frederic Taber Cooper, *The History of the Nineteenth Century in Caricature.* New York: Dodd, Mead, 1904.

Mayer, Henry (Hy), *Fantasies in Ha! Ha!* New York: Mayer, 1900.

Mellett, Lowell, "Herblock," *The New Republic,* May 17, 1954.

Mitchell, John Ames, "Contemporary American Caricature," *Scribner's Magazine,* Dec., 1889.

Monchak, Stephen J., "Thomas Nast's Fame Lives 100 Years After His Birth," *Editor & Publisher,* Sept. 28, 1940.

Morris, William C., *Spokesman-Review Cartoons.* Spokane: Review Publishing, 1908.

Mott, Frank Luther, *American Journalism.* New York, 1950.

——, *A History of American Magazines.* Cambridge: Harvard University Press, 1938–57, 4 vols.

Murrell, William, "Cartooning in Wartime America," *Art News,* Apr. 1–14, 1943.

——, *A History of American Graphic Humor, 1747–1865.* New York: Whitney Museum of American Art, 1933.

——, *A History of American Graphic Humor, 1865–1938.* New York: published for the Whitney Museum of American Art by Macmillan, 1938.

——, "Rise and Fall of Cartoon Symbols," *The American Scholar,* summer, 1935.

Nelan, Charles, *Cartoons of Our War with Spain.* New York: Stokes, 1898.

Nelson, Roy Paul, *Fell's Guide to the Art of Cartooning.* New York: Fell, 1962.

Neuberger, Richard L., "Hooverism in the Funnies," *The New Republic,* July 11, 1934.

Nevins, Allan, and Frank Weitenkampf, *A Century of Political Cartoons, Caricature in the United States from 1800 to 1900.* New York: Scribner's, 1944.

O'Connor, Richard, *The Scandalous Mr. Bennett.* Garden City, N.Y.: Doubleday, 1962.

O'Neil, William L., ed., *Echoes of Revolt: The Masses 1911–1917.* Chicago: Quadrangle, 1966.

Opper, Frederick, *Willie and His Papa.* New York: Grosset & Dunlap, 1901.

Paine, Albert Bigelow, *Th. Nast, His Period and His Pictures.* New York & London: Harper, 1904.

Parton, James, *Caricature and Other Comic Art in All Times and Many Lands.* New York: Harper, 1878.

Payne, Harold, "Our Caricaturists and Cartoonists," *Munsey's Magazine,* Feb., 1894.

"Pellegrini's Caricatures," *The Nation,* Apr. 11, 1872.

Penn, Arthur, "The Growth of Caricature," *The Critic,* Feb. 25, 1882.

Peters, Harry T., *Currier & Ives, Printmakers, to the American People*. Garden City, N.Y.: Doubleday, Doran, 1929 and 1931. 2 vols.

Pitney, A. de Ford, "O. Henry as a Cartoonist," *Cartoons Magazine*, Apr., 1917.

Raemakers, Louis, *America in the War*. New York: Century, 1918.

——, *Raemakers' Cartoon History of the War*. New York: Century, 1918.

——, *Raemakers' Cartoons*. Garden City, N.Y.: Doubleday, Page, 1917.

Red Cartoons from the Daily Worker. Chicago: Daily Worker, 1926.

Reed, Walt, ed., *The Illustrator in America 1900–1960s*. New York: Reinhold, 1966.

Renberg, Werner, "Old Man Texas Stands Up to Uncle Sam [John Knott]," *The Quill*, Apr., 1951.

Richardson, Frederick, *Book of Drawings*. Chicago: Lakeside Press, 1899.

——, "The Education of a Newspaper Artist," *The American Cartoonist Magazine*, Nov., 1903.

Ricker, Mary Swing, " 'Uncle Sam' in Cartoon," *The World To-Day*, Oct., 1910.

Robinson, Boardman, "America's Foremost Cartoonist Talks on Our Cartooning Art, and Tells Why It Misses Being Great," *Pep*, Nov., 1917.

——, *Cartoons on the War*. New York: Dutton, 1915.

——, *Ninety-Three Drawings*. Colorado Springs: Fine Arts Center, 1937.

Rogers, William A., *America's Black and White Book*. New York: Cupples & Leon, 1917.

——, *Hits at Politics*. New York: Russell, 1896.

——, *A World Worth While*. New York & London: Harper, 1922.

Rosenberg, Manuel, *Manuel Rosenberg Course in Cartooning*. Cincinnati: Manuel Rosenberg, 1927.

Russell, Ruth, "Orr-Cartoonist," *The Literary Digest*, May 30, 1925.

Rutledge, William A., III, "Dean of American Cartoonists [John T. McCutcheon]," *The Quill*, June, 1939.

——, "The Life Guard and the Lady [Vaughn Shoemaker]," *The Quill*, Sept., 1938.

Sasowsky, Norman, *Reginald Marsh*. New York: Praeger, 1956.

Saunders, John Monk, "This Cartoonist Gives Us a Look at Ourselves [H. T. Webster]," *The American Magazine*, Sept., 1924.

Schott, Henry, "J. N. Ding, Who Puts a Smile in Economics," *The Nation's Business*, May, 1925.

Shaw, Albert, *Abraham Lincoln*, New York: Review of Reviews, 1929. 2 vols.

——, *A Cartoon History of Roosevelt's Career*. New York: Review of Reviews, 1910.

Shelton, William Henry, "The Comic Paper in America," *The Critic*, Sept., 1901.

Sheridan, Martin, *Comics and Their Creators*. Hale, Cushman & Flint, 1942.

Shoemaker, Vaughn, *Cartoons by Vaughn Shoemaker*. Chicago: Chicago's American, n.d.

——, *1938 A.D.* Chicago: Daily News, 1939.

——, *1939 A.D.* Chicago: Daily News, 1940.

——, *1940 A.D.* Chicago: Daily News, 1941.

——, *'41 and '42 A.D.* Chicago: Daily News, 1942.

Smith, Beverly, "A Cartoonist Shows a State How to Enjoy Life [Jay N. Darling]," *The American Magazine,* Apr., 1933.

Smith, Dorman H., *One Hundred and One Cartoons.* Chicago: Ring, 1936.

Smith, Henry Ladd, "The Rise and Fall of the Political Cartoon," *Saturday Review,* May 29, 1954.

Smith, Katherine Louise, "Newspaper Art and Artists," *The Bookman,* Aug., 1901.

Spencer, Dick, III, *Editorial Cartooning.* Ames, Iowa: Iowa State College Press, 1949.

——, *Pulitzer Prize Cartoons.* Ames, Iowa: Iowa State College Press, 1951.

Szep, Paul. *In Search of Sacred Cows.* Boston: Boston *Globe,* 1968.

Thurber, James, *The Years with Ross.* Boston: Little, Brown, 1959.

Trumble, Alfred, "Satire, With Crayon and Pen," *The Epoch,* June 13, 1890.

Vinson, J. Chal, *Thomas Nast, Political Cartoonist.* Athens: University of Georgia Press, 1967.

Volck, A. J., "Confederate War Etchings," *The Magazine of History,* extra No. 60, 1917.

"W. A. Ireland Elected to Hall of Fame," *The Ohio Newspaper,* Oct., 1941.

Waldorf, A. Gayle, *Editor and Editorial Writer, Revised Edition.* New York: Rinehart, 1955.

Walker, Stanley, *City Editor.* New York: Stokes, 1934.

Walsh, William S., *Abraham Lincoln and the London Punch.* New York: Moffat, Yard, 1909.

Waugh, Coulton, *The Comics.* New York: Macmillan, 1947.

Weaver, John D., "Drawing Blood: Political Cartoonists," *Holiday,* Aug., 1915.

Webster, H. T., *The Best of H. T. Webster.* New York: Simon & Schuster, 1953.

Weiss, Harry B., *William Charles, Early Caricaturist, Engraver and Publisher of Children's Books.* New York: Public Library, 1932.

Weitenkampf, Frank, "American Cartoons of To-day," *Century,* Feb., 1913.

——, *American Graphic Art.* New York: Holt, 1912.

——, *Manhattan Kaleidoscope.* New York: Scribner's, 1947.

——, *Political Caricature in the United States in Separately Published Cartoons.* New York: Public Library, 1953.

——, "Political Cartoons as Historical Documents," *Bulletin of the New York Public Library,* Mar., 1946.

Westerman, Harry J., *A Book of Cartoons.* Columbus, Ohio: Edward T. Miller, n.d.

——, "Outlines Career of R. F. Outcault, Ohio-Born Artist," *The Ohio Newspaper,* Dec., 1933.

Westwood, H. R., *Modern Caricaturist.* London: Lovat Dickson, 1932.

Whitaker, J. V., "American Caricature," *Leisure Hour,* Sept. 30, Oct. 21, Nov. 25, and Dec. 16, 1876.

White, David Manning, *From Dogpatch to Slobbovia, The World of Li'l Abner.* Boston: Beacon, 1964.

White, David Manning, and Robert H. Abel, eds. *The Funnies, An American Idiom.* Glencoe, Ill.: Free Press, 1963.

White, Frank Linstow, "Some American Caricaturists," *The Journalist,* Nov. 19, 1887.

White, Richard Grant, "Caricature and Caricaturists," *Harper's Monthly Magazine,* Apr., 1862.

Widney, Gustavus C., "John T. McCutcheon, Cartoonist," *The World To-Day,* Oct., 1908.

Wilson, Rufus Rockwell, *Lincoln in Caricature.* New York: Horizon, 1953.

Wright, Grant, *The Art of Caricature.* New York: Baker Taylor, 1904.

Young, Art, *Art Young, His Life and Times.* New York: Sheridan House, 1939.

——, *The Best of Art Young.* New York: Vanguard, 1936.

——, *On My Way.* New York: Liveright, 1928.

Zimmerman, Eugene, *Cartoons and Caricatures.* Scranton, Pa.: Correspondence Institute of America, 1910.

——, "Rambles in Cartoondom," *Cartoons Magazine,* Nov., 1915, Apr. and Sept., 1916.

Index